"Prepare to have the dust shaken off of your religion. *The Courage to Be Queer* opens the tent of God's love to everybody by defying stereotypes and challenging biblical interpreters to be vital and alive. This book is an act of courage that calls upon people of faith to embrace their own personal difference and then act in freedom for the wellbeing of others. Jeff Hood says everyone is truly queer: unique, individual, and precious beyond all accounting to the Queer God who makes all people new in the Spirit. As Jeff Hood engages the world, Jesus Christ, and the most familiar stories from the Bible, he shows us how to discover anew the face of God in new forms of humanity and divinity. He is in the vanguard of a new spirituality for a new age. This is a must-read book!"

—**Rev. Dr. Stephen V. Sprinkle**, professor of Practical Theology, Brite Divinity School at Texas Christian University

"Reading Jeff Hood's work deepened my commitment to liberation theology and has firmly shifted my ambivalence about the word 'queer' to a place of tremendous pride in being queer. The real power in these words flows from the fact that Hood lives out the queer life he writes about."

—**Rev. Elder Jim Mitulski**, queer liberation activist and pastor in the Metropolitan Community Church, United Church of Christ, and Disciples of Christ denominations

"In imagining that great creative power we typically call God as 'the Queer,' Jeff Hood offers a radical vision where binaries of identity and reality no longer confine us. Hood's construction of this new liberation theology stands boldly in the tradition of other theologies that have expanded our understandings of who we are as individuals, as communities, and as spiritual beings, granting us a freedom to construct our lives and relationships in profoundly new ways. *The Courage to Be Queer* is a gift to all of us in our struggle to be fully human and fully free—fully queer!"

—**Rev. Kristin Stoneking**, executive director, Fellowship of Reconciliation

"The Queer is that which is not normative, the utterly unique. You would think that a law professor would have little use for the non-normative, especially when considered in the (for me) foreign context of "theology." I rummage through structures and norms for a living. It is precisely the point, however, that a theology that routinely and instinctively kills the 'Queer within' is no theology at all. Jeff Hood's exposition of theology is for everyone. Even someone as lost as me. For God is the ultimate Queer. Every page Jeff Hood has written is a step into the anti-conception and a step towards the non-normative power that is the reality most perfect for us to know of God. When I walk away from the normative, as Queer-protagonist, I am paradoxically walking towards the Queer-me that God has created. I am embracing the rubric of love by loving the Queer that is God, who is simultaneously embracing the Queer-me and helping me to see and embrace the Queer in others. The genius and pure light of this book is undeniable, and I cannot recommend it highly enough."

—**Michael C. Duff**, Centennial Distinguished Professor of Law,
University of Wyoming College of Law

"Buddhist and Christian literalisms often prevent us from perceiving the fundamental non-duality of the core teachings of both faith traditions: wisdom and compassion. Rev. Jeff Hood's *The Courage to Be Queer* is a timely and necessary exploration of the ultimate wisdom of interdependence and the radical compassion of acceptance of all differences as complementary aspects of ultimate reality. Christians will benefit from this incisive and faithful exploration of their Scriptures, and people of other faiths will be reminded of the need to appreciate and embrace difference in ourselves, our traditions, and our communities."

—**Ven. Tashi Nyima**, Nying Je Ling, Abode of Great Compassion,
New Jonang Buddhist Community

"How quickly we forget that we are 'a curious and peculiar people!' But Dr. Jeff Hood reminds us that in our unique individual stories of encounters with Holiness and discoveries of self, we find our splendid divine queerness and the wonder and liberation of the Queer Within. Bravo!"

—**Rev. Glenna Shepherd**, Pleasant Hill Community Church, United Church of Christ

"Queer theologies emerge from a variety of unexpected personal and social contexts. *The Courage to Be Queer* is the bold work of Baptist activist Jeff Hood."

—**Rev. Dr. Robert Shore-Goss**, pastor and theologian, Metropolitan Community Church United Church of Christ in the Valley, North Hollywood

"To be queer is to be authentically oneself—the self that God, the Ultimate Queer, longs for us to be. Reverend Dr. Jeff Hood, in his book, *The Courage to Be Queer*, has brought his own queries and queering to Scripture in order to free us all from the bonds of normativity. Mixing exegetical reflection and an earthy practical theology, Hood offers the church a broader vision of the Divine . . . inviting us to reclaim what is queerest and best about our story and to see how our lives, in all their uniqueness, comprise God's story in this world."

—**Rev. Ashlee Wiest-Laird**, pastor of First Baptist Church in Jamaica Plain, Massachusetts

"Through bold interpretation of Scripture and gentle vulnerability, Jeff Hood masterfully reminds us that normativity is the great sin of our time."

—**Rev. Justin Hancock**, author and disability theologian, Missional Wisdom Foundation

"Jeff Hood's new book, *The Courage to Be Queer*, is both queer and courageous. Hood expands on our understanding of queer identity to see it as a category of liberation open to anyone who is willing to let go of their fears and connect with what is most sacred and most true in their being. When we do that, he suggests, we are in a position to change the world. Hood intriguingly turns the table on our typical reactions to what is marginalized in our culture as that which should be discounted, pitied, or shunned. For Hood it is in these places of difference where we can find an authentic spirituality that speak to our core being. From such places, a revitalized Christian theology is possible that can embrace what is best, most wild, and most queer in us."

—**Dr. Sharon Groves**, faith organizer and social justice worker

"*The Courage to Be Queer* is a challenging read—not for the weak of mind or spirit. For Hood this is a theological, heartfelt exercise of courage genuinely rooted in his love of all humanity. This love envelopes his more normative conservative friends on one end all the way to his associates uninvited to sit in traditional pews. I invite you to get lost in Hood's use of the word 'Queer' and explore this path of salvation."

—**Rev. Duncan E. Teague**, Unitarian Universalist minister and faith outreach consultant, Georgia Equality

"Dr. Hood's explorations of the Queer are relevant, raw, and liberating. His writing led me to question my own limited constructs in ways that stretched and then freed me. His book is an experience of self-discovery and a courageous revelation of love."

—**Dr. Celeste Holbrook**, sexual health educator and consultant

"One of the great challenges of youth ministry is helping young people embrace the unique person God is calling them to be. Dr. Hood's *The Courage to Be Queer* offers a clear path for radical dialogue that will lead to radical spaces of openness, inclusion, and empowerment. If you want to learn how to change the world, read this book!"

—**Jason Redick**, youth minister, Holy Covenant United Methodist Church

"Jeff Hood's book is a thoughtful and personal theological manifesto in the best Baptist traditions of soul freedom and liberation. I'm excited to be a part of some of the conversations this book starts!"

—**Rev. David Weasley**, board chair, Association of Welcoming and Affirming Baptists

"Radical, readable, and intellectually rigorous, *The Courage to be Queer* by Jeff Hood reveals a theology of God the Queer that speaks to everyone through their individual context or queerness. The author does an extraordinary job of making advanced theological concepts accessible and inviting—all with sound biblical references. Hood shakes the demons out of the Bible and leaves only love."

—**Rev. Kittredge Cherry**, author and founder of Jesusinlove.org

"Jeff Hood reminds us that theology is based in story. *The Courage to Be Queer* is filled with stories of life-giving liberation. Hood brings the resurrection close and knocks the cobwebs out of obsolete theologies traditionally used to demean and diminish to better remind us of our own uniqueness or queerness. This book has rebooted my allegiance to the inclusive, compassionate, radically creative, and loving God who truly is the queerest of the queer."

—**Rev. Mike Wright-Chapman**, associate pastor, Cathedral of Hope United Church of Christ

"Reverend Hood displays a strong courage to take on tough tasks. It doesn't get any tougher than exploring the queerness of the church and people of faith. By taking a term of derision, 'queer,' and using it analyze our place in the universe, Hood pushes us to think theologically and have our lives transformed by the results. I dare you to read this book."

—**Rev. David W. Key Sr.**, director of Baptist Studies, Candler School of Theology at Emory University

"Jeff writes with a prophetic edge, refreshing vulnerability, and deep theological reflection. His exploration of queer theology is rooted in his commitment to all of God's children. This book offers an engaging approach to anyone who wishes to learn and understand more about the queer within and around us."

—**Rev. Leah Grundset Davis**, communications specialist, Alliance of Baptists

"*The Courage to Be Queer* is a theological exploration that is both universal and particular. Through personal story and cogent exegesis, Jeff Hood moves 'queer' from a derogatory slur to an identity that goes beyond sexuality to any expression of otherness separating us from the love of God."

—**Chett Pritchett**, executive director, Methodist Federation for Social Action

"There are few voices in the Christian world like that of the Reverend Dr. Jeff Hood. He has the heart of a pastor, the voice of a prophet, the mind of a scholar, and the temperament of a servant leader. These qualities, along with his keen spiritual insight, are on full display within this text. His writing has the unique ability to see the Divine in new and fresh ways while challenging his reader with both love and boldness. I encourage every reader to approach this work with a hunger and thirst for transformation. For if you remain open to the moving of God's spirit, the transformation of heart and mind will indeed be yours. So, be ready for a journey . . . the journey of the remarkable . . . the journey of the queer. For it's within the queer that presence of God can be found!"

—**Rev. Ray Jordan**, Central Congregational Church, United Church of Christ

"*The Courage to Be Queer* is a call to move into the transformation and liberation of God. The queer narrative Jeff shares pushes us to stretch, heal, and cultivate our theology and our hearts."

—**Kathy McDougall**, pastor and community curator at Zeteo Houston

"I couldn't put Dr. Hood's *The Courage to Be Queer* down! Declaring a vision for radical inclusivity, Dr. Hood beautifully pushes through normative closets and breathes sincerity, passion, and generosity anew into faith. His personal narrative, interwoven with biblical hermeneutic and liberation theology, invites the reader into God's world, where no one is left out at the table of love. While there will be some who say this book is too radical, I left the book encouraged boldly encouraged to stand for truth, justice, and love."

—**Rev. Kyle Lee Tubbs**, pastor and planter, Grace Baptist Church in Round Rock, Texas

"Life takes courage . . . courage to know your story, courage to share your story, and courage to hear the stories of others. But the deepest courage comes when we try to connect our story with the stories of others. As Jeff so poignantly shares in *The Courage to Be Queer*, we all exist and seek meaning from within our own person. When we learn to exist and seek meaning through our human uniqueness or queerness, we learn to push back against the normative forces that hold us back. This is a text that helps us learn to dance."

—**Rev. Dr. John Casimir O'Keefe**, author and lead pastor, Cross Bridge Christian Church, Disciples of Christ

"How refreshing! God is not trapped in worn-out rhetoric, nor in crumbling edifices. The Holy Spirit is not tongue-tied to speak only old conclusions. Yes, yes, this book is Queer, and I love its Gospel Truth."

—**Dr. Louie Crew**, professor emeritus at Rutgers University and founder of Integrity: A Ministry of LGBTQ Episcopalians

"*The Courage to Be Queer* is a powerful book that invites readers to consider theology, the world, and themselves beyond the confines of tradition. In doing so, our understanding of self is allowed to develop as a reflection of a diverse and loving God. We all can find courage through Jeff's words."

—**Rev. Maurice "Bojangles" Blanchard**, Baptist minister and plaintiff in Bourke v. Beshear, the 2015 United States Supreme Court same-sex marriage case

"In *The Courage to Be Queer*, Jeff takes the little mental closet that we have tried to contain God within and smashes it wide open. Armed with his own spiritual journey and a queer hermeneutic, Jeff boldly proclaims good news to the poor, binds up the brokenhearted, releases captives and prisoners, and announces the year of the Lord's favor. Jeff believes in a God who is wilder, freer, and more loving than many of us have dared to imagine. This book made me blush, made me question why I was blushing, and freed me to accept myself a little bit more."

—**Dan Kiniry**, founder and pastor, Neal Park Potluck

"Jeff Hood is an extraordinary theologian who uses precision mixed with creativity to elevate the theological discourse. Hood's determination to intersect theology and praxis through activism demands our attention to his prophetic voice."

—**Rev. Mitchell Boone**, White Rock United Methodist Church

"Like Jeff, I too believe that queerness is not just a legitimate identity to be defended but a vocation for all of us to learn. This a text that will help us on the journey."

—**Rev. Morgan Guyton**, director of NOLA Wesley Foundation, United Methodist Church

"This text is an authentically queer spiritual and intellectual journey into the depths of what it means to be both fully human and fully created in the image of the Divine that leads to delight and hope for us all."

—**Sarah Griffith Lund**, author of *Blessed Are the Crazy: Breaking the Silence about Mental Illness, Family, and Church*

"*The Courage to Be Queer* is a theological masterpiece. Jeff Hood weaves a brilliant tapestry of God's love. This text is the answer for anyone struggling to believe God loves all people."

—**Rev. Donald H. Fulton**, Alliance of Baptists

"As a cis-hetero ally to LGBT neighbors, I carried on a 'compassionate' conversation about 'them' until I met Rev. Dr. Hood. In his preaching, his way of being, and his scholarship he showed me that there is no 'them' — or rather, that we are all 'other,' all queer, and all beloved by our God who is Other, who is Queer, who loves beyond our ridiculous differentiations. Jeff offered me the courage to be queer, a good gift for which I'm grateful."

—**Rev. Dr. Katie Hayes**, Galileo Church (Disciples of Christ)

The Courage to Be Queer

The Courage to Be Queer

Jeff Hood

FOREWORD
Brandan Robertson

AFTERWORD
Kim Jackson

Dan! Thank you for your consistent work. Keep it QUEER!

+ JEFF

WIPF & STOCK · Eugene, Oregon

THE COURAGE TO BE QUEER

Wipf & Stock
An Imprint of Wipf and Stock Publishers
199 W. 8th Ave., Suite 3
Eugene, OR 97401

www.wipfandstock.com

ISBN 13: 978-1-4982-2191-7

Manufactured in the U.S.A.   09/09/2015

For the Queers

Contents

Foreword

WHEN I THINK OF Jeff Hood, I think of John the Baptist. A wild-eyed, bearded preacher standing on the outskirts of town preaching the radical message that God is doing a new thing in our day. Crowds flock to hear the message he has to proclaim. Many religious leaders were infuriated by what John had to say. Many of the devout were confused. But the marginalized heard hope in his voice. They saw liberation on the horizon. For them, this unkempt holy man was a sign that a new day was about to break forth in their world. It is in that same unkempt spirit that Rev. Jeff Hood appears on the scene. Standing on the outside of the church, calling to those on the inside to come and taste the kingdom of God that is manifesting just beyond their line of sight.

My first interaction with Jeff Hood came in fall of 2014 as I was working to launch an organization called Evangelicals for Marriage Equality. On the week of our public launch, I received an email from Jeff that said, "I don't know whether or not I should be excited for your new organization." I had never met Jeff before but was intrigued by his forwardness. We began discussing, first via email and then on the phone, our common journey from conservative evangelicalism to a more progressive faith. The more we talked, the more I became intrigued by Jeff's unique theological perspective. But I didn't realize just how *queer* Jeff's theology was until a few weeks later, when he invited me to speak at his home congregation in Texas. Over the course of the weekend, Jeff and I spent many late nights and many long rides in the car debating, discussing, and dissecting our theological perspectives on sexuality and gender identity. Jeff articulated his unique theological position, rooted in queer theory, liberation theology, and also a distinctly Southern Baptist evangelical theology in a way that captured my attention. I had never imagined that a single theologian could incorporate three traditions that are totally distinct and in many ways opposed to one another to create such a beautiful theological portrait of what it means to be truly human—made in the image and likeness of God. But Jeff's theology didn't really grip me until I saw it in action.

On my first night in Texas, Jeff drove me to a local hospital for a pastoral visit to a young gay man in his congregation who had attempted suicide earlier that week. As Jeff and I walked into the hospital room where this man lay heavily sedated, I watched Jeff approach the bedside, grip this man's cold hand, and begin to pray. He prayed that this man would be healed, not only in his body or mind, but also in the way that he perceived himself. He prayed that this man would learn to walk in his *unique* or *queer* identity, embracing the whole of who God made him to be. I looked at the pale face of this brother who had been stricken with so much grief and I saw just how real and how needed Jeff's theology was. A word of liberation was needed. A word of affirmation was needed. A word of love was needed. And Jeff's vision of queerness offers that to the world.

There is a whole group of gender non-conforming individuals and sexual minorities who live in a world that teaches them to conform to a label or culturally constructed identity. If they don't conform, they are marginalized, oppressed, and chastised. This is still a reality in our secular society today and it is most certainly a reality in the Church of Jesus Christ. Those who claim to be followers of the radically unique and unconditionally inclusive Son of God have become a force of oppression and abuse to countless individuals God has made with a unique sexual orientation or gender identity. In the church, all action is driven by our theology. The church oppresses sexual minorities because its theology leads it to do so. In every generation, God raises up prophetic voices that speak an unpopular word to God's people, calling them forward to come closer to the full revelation of God's kingdom. For our age,

Rev. Jeff Hood is truly one of those voices, speaking a vitally important word to the church that calls us to reform our beliefs about sexuality and gender identity and to repent of the oppression we have perpetuated.

I have seen Jeff live this theology out. I have watched as he articulated his queer vision of God to some of the most prominent Christian leaders of our day and seen how their thinking began to shift as they considered what Jeff had to say. Jeff's theology is radical, to be sure. But it is also one of the most liberating perspectives I have ever come across. Parts of Jeff's teaching have affected the way I view myself, my relationship with God, and how I interact with the wide array of unique individuals that surround me each and every day.

In the pages of this book, you will find some of the most compelling and simultaneously challenging theology you have ever encountered. You will likely disagree with some of what you read and feel compelled to take a defensive posture against the queer perspective of God that Jeff is articulating. But I encourage you to come to this text with an open heart and a prayerful attitude, expecting to have your theological paradigm turned upside down. Come to this text with a spirit of exploration, expecting to be pushed to see things in a whole new light and go willingly into uncharted territory. For it is in these uncomfortable spaces that our eyes can be opened to see God in new and exciting ways. Come to this text not only willing to learn, also but willing to grow deeper in to your own identity as a queer child of God and in your relationship with your Creator.

I have known few scholars, pastors, and friends as innovative, caring, and brilliant as Jeff Hood. I have known no one as courageous. A prophet is never received in his hometown, as the saying goes, but his word is always timely. Jeff Hood has proven his unwavering faith in God and his commitment to living out the radical implications of the gospel time and time again through his dedication to uplifting the marginalized at immense personal cost. And as difficult as it may be to be a prophet to a new generation, no one is better equipped for the job than Jeff Hood. In these pages you will hear his message. Open your hearts. Expand your mind. Receive the new word God is speaking to you today.

Prepare to be transformed.

—**Brandan Robertson**

National Spokesperson for Evangelicals
for Marriage Equality

February 2015

Preface

THEOLOGY IS BASED IN story. In stories we find the epicenter of queerness. No two stories are exactly the same. In the midst of the pursuit of meaning, most of us look to the world to give us answers. We place our person in categories and identities to define who we are and what God is.[1] The sinfulness of such a method is that it assumes that the meaning of the self or God comes from somewhere other than within. We are unique queers created in the image of a God who is queer beyond our normative constructions.[2] God the Queer lives in our queer stories. The Queer is always connected to our own experiences. How could the Queer not be? We all exist and seek meaning from within our own person. In this life, we will never know the eternal fullness of the Queer within, because we don't have the knowledge of eternal fullness of the meaning of past, present, or future, but we never stop seeking. Queering consistently unsettles in order to point to something far beyond our normative constructions. In our unsettling exploration, we begin the journey to become the fullness of the Queer in whose image we are made.

Though no two explorations are ever the same, this project is intended to offer the reader an example of what a radical queer orthodoxy grounded in the self can look like when we take the discovery and experience of the Queer within and apply it to

1. The use of the term "we" throughout this project does not mean that I assume all readers are in agreement with me. I use it out of a sense of formality and as an invitation for readers to "think with" me on this theological journey.

2. A constructive understanding of this identifier will be discussed further into the introduction.

Scripture. There will be those who question my emphasis on Scripture; I don't blame them. Throughout my life, I have seen Scripture used to normatize, manipulate, and control. For those who are skeptical, I invite you to think about this project as an exorcism. I am queering the fundamental religious text of my spiritual tradition in order to shake the demons out. Queering is a means of exorcism. We exorcise the normative, or sin, in order to remove all obstacles to the Queer. We begin with the normative obstacles in our own experiences. I can think of no more normative of an obstacle in my life to the Queer than Scripture.

The queer approach I take is an invitation for others to join me. I seek to encourage others to explore and interact with the queer moments in their lives to create queer lenses that can help them better understand themselves and the world around them. When we begin to allow the self to be queered and we work to queer the world around us, we start to create honest community and social change based on difference rather than normative constructions of sameness. In queering the world, we begin the process of removing all obstacles to the Queer and each other. Though my story and exploration are queer to me, I long for this project to provide exemplification and inspiration for others to begin their own queer theological explorations. In the unity of the exploration of our queerness, I believe we can excise the demons in us and resurrect the Queer in our world.

—**Rev. Dr. Jeff Hood**

February 2015

Acknowledgments

LIKE ANYTHING WORTH A shit, a great cloud of people worked together to help me produce *The Courage to Be Queer*. Some people knew they helped me, and some people helped by accident.

I must thank those who worked hard to keep me closeted my whole life. Those who told me to be silent, thank you for helping me to find the courage to speak. Those who told me to stop, thank you for teaching me that truth always marches on. Those who pushed me to go in a different direction, thank you for encouraging me to listen to the voice of God alone.

While it always sounds award-showish, I have to thank God. If the Queer had not knocked on the door of my closet, I never would have made it. God sent some angels who have helped me along the way. Frances taught me the fortitude of Jesus. Johnny taught me how to have courage like Jesus. Jackie taught me how to listen like Jesus. Charles taught me the compassion of Jesus. Steve taught me how to think like Jesus. Jim taught me how to love like Jesus. Duncan taught me the grace of Jesus. Tashi reinforced the pacifism of Jesus. Knowing that I have met God through them, I am beyond thankful for these queer Jesus impersonators.

One cannot make it in this life without friends. When most of my childhood and college friends abandoned me due to my increasingly queer activism and theology, Stephen and Kathleen were always there to cheer me on. Lanie continued to grow up with me. When I was at my lowest at the unbelievably normative Southern Baptist Theological Seminary, Don came out to me and taught me to not be afraid anymore. When I got to Emory University and had few friends, Lucas befriended me and never let me go. Over the last few years, Dave filled the role of my comrade on the West Coast. Through it all, Tyler was and is there for the laughs.

Liz, Kathy, and Jason have read almost everything that I have written over the last few years. I am a better writer and theologian because they live. I am so grateful for each of their friendships. I promise to keep sending you stuff.

For the last two years, I have visited Will on Texas' death row. Throughout our visits, I have learned what it looks like to embrace the queerness of life no matter the circumstance. During the same time, Broderick has also been a steady companion in a variety of settings, and I am thankful for his friendship.

Brandan taught me that evangelicalism still has room for some queers. Danny pushed me to sit at the table every once in a while. Kim and Trina consistently bless me with the strength of their wisdom and guidance. Glenna, Kyndra, and Andy are queers in action. Matt came back. Martin and Malcolm never leave me. Francisco, Mitchell, and Justin discussed the ideas of this project with me over and over. I am very grateful for each of their imprints on this project.

There are so many friends that I just don't have the room to name. You know who you are, and you are loved.

Before I thank my family, I must thank Wipf & Stock for taking a chance on a crazy queer book like this. I also am thankful for the guidance and friendship of Christian in the submission of this project and the amazing editorial work of Alex. This book is because all of you are.

Families are always complicated. Though my paternal grandparents are dead and were very conservative in life, I inherited a tremendous legacy of faith. My maternal grandparents will never understand why I would publish such a book, but I could not have made it through school without their help. I will be forever grateful for the inheritances of faith and education from my grandparents.

For most of my life, my mom and I have struggled greatly. Regardless, I love her and she has always loved me. I would never have developed the insatiable thirst for knowledge that produced this book without her guidance. My dad taught me that people

Acknowledgments

matter. In his regular giving of his life for people, Dad showed me what a real hero is. Since I held him for the first time, Justin Hood has been my best friend. I am thankful for my complicated family.

Words do not exist to describe how much I love Emily Jean Hood. Ours is the love beyond love. This is Emily's book. Without Emily, I could have never written anything like this. Emily is my muse . . . the queerest woman I know.

Jeffrey Kyle Hood III, Phillip Ray Emory Hood, Quinley Mandela Dillard Hood, Oscar Lucas Campbell Hood, and Madeleine Jean Frances Hood, your daddy loves you more than the reach of the entire universe. I will forever fight for the space for you to be the queers that God has created you to be. This is your book for your future. Open the door!

Introduction

THEOLOGY WITHOUT THE PRACTICAL is dead, and dead theologies do not bring about resurrection. I seek theology that speaks life into death. I believe there is desperate need for a universal theology that can exist among and participate with other theologies and speak resurrection to the entire breadth of human uniqueness or queerness. That is what this project is about. It is my intention to develop a theology of queerness using a queer hermeneutic that is based on a core understanding that human beings are created uniquely queer in the image of a God who is queer and that resurrection comes through the discovery of the Queer within and without. This theology is an attempt to correct the efforts of the church to tame or shun the Queer. I propose that salvation can be found nowhere but the Queer. I am attempting to redefine in a radically inclusive way what it means to follow God. The core of this theology is that the Queer within us is the source from which flows all knowledge of the Queer. When we claim who we are as a unique, queer, individual made by a God who is queer, we are each creating the needed space within our self to interact with the divine within our self. The Queer is the source of universal liberation because the Queer calls all to move beyond the yoke of trying to be something other than queer or what God created us to be. This is a theology of individual liberation. In this queer space of discovery and freedom, I believe that we are finally able to blur constructed and normatized identities to move to a place of acknowledgment that all people are unique, queer individuals made in the image of God and worthy of the individual resurrection of acceptance, community, and love. This is a theology of discovery and reconstruction. This is the story of God

1

drawing queer to queer and queering the world with acceptance through difference and love.

The Courage to Be Queer is an intricate dance between hermeneutical interpretation and theological exploration.[1] Throughout this introduction, I will prepare the path for a wider journey into both the chosen self and the chosen texts. In relating personal experience, creating new terminology, and exploring past hermeneutics and theology, I will describe the experiential epiphany of the Queer within me that brought me to this place of hermeneutical and theological construction.

As much as I wish it was not so and that God-talk could exist beyond language, theology has to be constructed using language, and thus terms are important. In "The Start" I discuss where the idea for this project came from. In "Terms of Description," I explain how I use language to describe my experiences and to construct this work of queer theology.[2] It is not lost on me that the word "queer" does not appear in the majority of mainstream translations of Scripture, but I think there are plenty of words and ideas that can be reinterpreted and reimagined to discover the queer within Scripture. In "The Queer Theological Approach," I illustrate and explicate the reinterpretive theological approach taken in the construction of this project. In a paraphrase of the writer of Ecclesiastes, it is important to remember "there is nothing new under the sun" (1:9).[3] In "Precursors Descending," I illustrate where I see this project falling into the long history of hermeneutical and theological adaptation and reinterpretation. In the conclusion of the introduction and in the beginning of the wider work, I briefly outline the chapters of the project in "The Epiphany of the Queer."

1. The diversity of other studies that combine hermeneutical interpretation and theological exploration will be explored deeper into the introduction.

2. The tactic of self-assertion and self-introjection is a primary strategy of contextual theological hermeneutics.

3. Though I begin with the New Revised Standard Version (NRSV) of Scripture throughout this work, I use it to relay the meaning of Scripture in a variety of ways. Sometimes I use the straight rendering. Sometimes I use a paraphrase. Sometimes I use an adaptation. Regardless of where I end up, the NRSV is where I begin.

Introduction

The Start

I once led a private time of sharing and healing for victims of spiritual violence. Paul walked in and took his seat near the back of the room. After a couple of people told a few stories of harsh evangelical backgrounds, Paul spoke up and described being probed in his anus by members of his Roman Catholic youth group. The intention of the attack was to show Paul how painful being queer could be. People consistently ask me how anyone can morally claim to act in the name of Jesus when such atrocities and violence are consistently committed against queer folk in the name of Jesus. My gut reply surprises everyone, "We have to kill Jesus." It is an epiphany that has been a lifetime in the making. Unless the Jesus or God of tradition dies, then a God that is as real and queer as us cannot be resurrected. In these moments of epiphany I consistently meet the Queer, but such moments originate in a journey.

Life is filled with experiences of people trying to squash what God has created each of us to be. Religion is one of the chief vehicles used to corrupt the Queer image of God in all people. I come from a Southern Baptist background and was ordained as a Southern Baptist minister. I know a thing or two about religious normatization. My people have attempted to use God, Jesus, salvation, ethics, sexuality, gender, family values, and a whole host of other things to bludgeon people into normative constructs created to control. In my time as a student at the Southern Baptist Theological Seminary, my heart was crushed by normative constructions on many occasions. Perhaps the chief occasion occurred when one of my closeted fellow students asked a professor what to do if they could not shake their attraction to the same sex. The professor said to pray for death, for it is better to die than live in sin. Needless to say, the professor was attempting to bully the student out of two of God's most precious gifts: his life and his sexuality. Oppression is an incredibly normative construct. When we realize the queer that we are created by God to be, those who try to steal our queerness from us become not just obstacles in the short term, but the very enemies of God.

In retrospect, I realize that I have journeyed toward the Queer within. The traditional boundaries and identities contained in typical God–talk feel uncomfortable and oppressive. There was always an attempt to control. I found God to be a God of love and freedom, Jesus being the chief expression of such. I, however, always felt like something was missing—something was not right. I discovered the source of my angst when I encountered queer communities fighting the church for the right to express the Queer within. Many of these individuals were lesbian, gay, bisexual, or transgender, but many were not. All were fighting to be able to be who God created them to be. I knew that this was my struggle too: to be who God created me to be. The God who describes God's self as "I AM" forty-three different places in the Hebrew Bible (e.g., Exod 3:14; Gen 26:3; Zech 8:8), was calling me to the same level of acceptance of whose and who I was: "I AM" queer. When I found myself in the community called queer, I found God as well. The traditional boundaries began to change. Queerness was no longer something to be frightened of; it was something to be sought, embraced, and expressed. It was divine.

Terms of Description

It is my intention to use a queer hermeneutic to develop a queer theology that speaks to all individuals through their individual context or queerness. Throughout this project, I will define queer using a primary definition of that which is non-normative. I see normativity as synonymous with evil or sin. The creation myth provides a beautiful introduction to this concept. The serpent informs Eve in Gen 3:4 that if you eat of the fruit, "you will be made like God." In turn, the metaphorical fall cannot simply be described as an act of disobedience, as this fails to capture the total illustrative nature of the passage. The fall is both Adam and Eve's rejection of the God within, or the unique queer individual they were created by God to be, in order to chase the false normative construction of God created by the serpent. This resistance reading of Genesis sees the rejection of the queer individuals God has created us to be as the original sin.[4]

The level of acceptance or rejection of queerness is best measured using the rubric of love. This rubric can be described on multiple levels based on six theological presuppositions.

First, to reject the Queer within is to reject God. To love the Queer within is to love God. Rejection of the Queer within leads to a rejection of the Queer in the other.

Second, to reject the Queer in the other is to reject the God in the other. To love the Queer in the other is to love the God in the other. Rejection of the Queer in the other leads to a rejection of the Queer in communities.

Third, to reject the Queer in communities is to reject the God in communities. To love the Queer in communities is to love the God in communities. Rejection of the Queer in communities leads to the rejection of peoples.

Fourth, to reject the Queer in peoples is to reject the God in peoples. To love the Queer in peoples is to love the God in peoples. Rejection of the Queer in peoples leads to the rejection of the Queer in the world.

Fifth, to reject the Queer in the world is to reject the God in the world. To love the Queer in the world is to love the God in the world. Rejection of the Queer in the world leads to the rejection of the Queer in the universe.

Sixth, rejection of the Queer in the universe leads to the rejection of the God in the universe. To love the Queer in the universe is to love the God in the universe. Rejection of the Queer in the universe begins with the rejection of the Queer within. Rejection of the Queer in the universe also leads to the rejection of the Queer within. To reject the Queer in the other, communities, peoples, the world, or the universe is to reject the Queer within.

A belief in the intersectionality of all things is vitally important to this construction of queer theology. Love of the Queer within and without begins with understanding the intersectionality of

---

4. For more on the approach of resistance reading, see Tolbert, *Bible and Feminist Hermeneutics*.

all things and seeking to love all things. Rejection is the antithesis of love, and to reject the Queer is not to love. To reject love is to reject God.

If the antithesis of love is rejection, then love itself can be understood primarily by the sacrifice of acceptance. It is important to note that it does take sacrifice to practice acceptance. To accept the Queer within, we must sacrifice the constructs of normativity that our minds are bombarded with every day through messages that try to convince us that who we are is not good enough. To accept the other, communities, peoples, the world, and the universe, we have to sacrifice the security of non-engagement or isolation. These acceptances are all interconnected. The more we are able to accept the world without, the more we are able to accept the world within. If you want to heal yourself, then you are going to have to love somebody. If you want to heal the world, then you are going to have to love somebody. Love begins and ends with the sacrificial act of acceptance.

In Mark 12:30–31, Jesus says that one should "love . . . God with all your heart, and with all your soul, and with all your mind, and with all your strength . . . You shall love your neighbor as yourself." To love God, or the Queer, we must push past normative constructions about meaning and value in this life, which often deprive us of being the Queer within we were created to be. To love the neighbor as the self, we must sacrifice our hesitancy to accept or find the Queer within the other. We must value the Queer in the other as much as we value the Queer within ourselves. Jesus, in John 15:13, states, "Greater love has no one than this, to lay down one's life for one's friends." It seems that we cannot lay something down of our own accord unless we know what we are laying down. There is a need to know the Queer in order to give or sacrifice the Queer. One must know the self in order to give or sacrifice the self. In 1 Cor 13, Paul states, "the greatest of these is love." In the end, though there will be other constructs remaining, love is the greatest. If 1 John 4:8 is correct and "God is love," then love and God are inextricably linked. Love will always be non-normative or queer in a world of insecurity, violence, and hate. Love will be God, and the greatest measure of that which is queer is God. Queerness functions as that which powers love and, consequently, life. Fitting ways of talking about our experience of this amalgamation of divinity might be: Queer the universe, love. Queer the world, love. Queer your community, love. Queer your self, love. The mystery (or that which is beyond our normative explanations) explodes from the activity of love, which is the very queer creator or core of the universe.

Theologies are constructed from an individual point in time and should speak beyond time. Traditions and histories inform theologies, and this theology will be no different. I will begin the construction of this theology in a place of perfection and conclude in a place of perfection. Perfection, or eschatological hope, is at the core construction of this theology.

The Queer Theological Approach

To pursue holiness is to pursue Godliness. That which is holy is that which is most intimately connected to God. The Queer within is the image of the God who made us. Holiness is the pursuit of the Queer, or God. Queerness is a recognition and pursuit of the God within and without. Queerness and holiness are ultimately synonymous terms. Holiness is pursued and found from where you are—your context.

Since the beginning, theology has always been constructed in context. We speak from where we are. We are always seeking, wondering, loving, fighting, and dreaming from our own time and our location. We raise our voices to speak, to name who and where we are. We wander and grope in the darkness to find the God who made us. We love each other in hopes that we might touch something eternal and transcendent by sharing love. We fight for a more just world because we believe justice is possible. We dream of a world made whole because there is something in us that believes that once, in a faraway place, wholeness was real and perhaps wholeness might be made real again. In a world being slowly demoralized by oppression, those of us who theologize in context choose to believe that there is hope for our local and global community and for us. Theology is an exercise of contextual hope. We are not alone in our efforts, as the consistent incarnation of God in Jesus is the ultimate expression of the continual creation of contextual hope.

In Matt 25:35–36 and 40, Jesus makes it quite clear where the incarnational context of Jesus or God will always be: "I was hungry and you gave me food, I was thirsty and you gave me drink, I was a stranger and you welcomed me, naked and you gave me clothing, sick and in prison and you visited me . . . Truly I tell you, just as you did it to one of the least of these, you did it to me."[5] In the context of the consistent denial of rights, the consistent hate crimes, the consistent religious violence, and other marginalizations committed against those we call non-normative or lacking in their ability to fit our categories or idealizations of acceptance, it seems quite obvious to me that queer folk, or those who defy normatized constructions, are indeed the least of these. The location of the Queer is where we need to go to find God and any constructions of theology that might follow.

In order to arrive at the place where we can look to the Queer to create theology, something must die—namely, rigid normative traditional concepts that are consistently used to oppress. I have often found that traditional concepts of God do not allow room for expressing humanity's varied experiences of God. Death is not something to be feared, as I do not believe in death without resurrection; things die and create new life. God in Jesus gives up life so that life may be made full. There is a sense in which God is consistently giving and receiving life. The danger of traditional

5. I read the Bible within and out of my context. I seek to allow the Bible to speak to and challenge me within and without to be a better Christian. The approach I employ is one that many liberation popular theologians use to correlate the world of the text with the world in front of the text. This approach is ideological in orientation, which desacrilizes the normativity of the text using the experience of the reader. For instance, if Jesus says that Jesus will inhabit the least, then I seek to find the least around me and go where they are so that the God who inhabits the least might touch me and the God who inhabits me might touch the least. This is the way I find God in the Bible.

theologians is their unwillingness to open up to the possibility that God's death and resurrection is the true path to loving acceptance of queerness in the self, each other, the world, and in the divine.

Theology must be contextual, but contextual categories can only take us so far in our attempts to reach a place where we recognize the God within and without. We must realize that context comes from the individual, and therefore theology must spring from the individual. Genesis 1:27 purports that we are created in the very image of God. This means that every human being is a unique reflection of God. It is important to state that God is black. It is important to state that God is brown. It is important to state that God is a lesbian. It is important to state that God is intersex. It is important to state that God is disabled. It is important to say all of these things and more because the individual is important. Constructions of shared identities can help us to understand God, but we must push further. We need to push to a place where we can discover the source of the whole of humanity by championing the uniqueness of the individual so that we may proceed to a place of community constructed in difference. There is something uniting and guiding us, something that draws each of us deep within the self so that we might discover the creator and sustainer of the universe.

There is a need for sacrifice and death in order that we might find the uniquely non-normative source and sum of the entirety of all uniquely non-normative creations. It is irreparably harmful to say that God loves someone but hates a core biological part of who they are. It is divisive and unhelpful to argue that a certain identity characteristic makes one superior to anyone else. No matter the source, words of oppression are shallow and have never made sense. There is a deep need to create a theology that celebrates the unique dignity and worth of all people as individuals so that unique individuals can come together to create honest community. I am interested in a theology that can speak to a woman I met not long ago. She was the product of four different races—her mother was of Mexican and Japanese descent and her father was of Irish and Ghanaian descent—and she also identified as a lesbian. When I told her that I was a pastor, she asked me bluntly, "I have wondered my whole life, where do I fit?" One of the great tasks I seek to accomplish in this project is creating a theology that allows such a woman to be the unique, non-normative creation of God she was born to be in her context. I believe if God is near and here in the diversity represented in every individual, then surely God must be queer.

A resurrection of theology requires a willingness to deconstruct and let die traditional and modern concepts that do not allow room for the Queer, or God. New constructions and ways of thinking must give way to experimental constructions of hope and promise. In the gospels, Jesus consistently deconstructs the egotistical religion. Jesus takes things even further by placing the center of spiritual life outside the normative gates, squarely in the midst of those people a society of boundaries has left out, marginalized, and oppressed. We must stand with Jesus against efforts to divide and disenfranchise by firmly creating theology that upholds the inherent worth of each individual at their core. I am simply no longer comfortable using the same constructions of theology that were used to lock out, deny communion, and brutalize those people deemed out-of-bounds or non-normative by our churches. The theological resurrection I have experienced continues to come in the presence of a God who dares to be queer by God's very nature and calls us to the same.

Precursors Descending

The theological question of the meaning of the individual as context and source in relation to God descends from a long line of non-conformist theologies and thoughts. In the following study, I will not only show that my line of questioning and constructivist queer theology is not new, but also that it aligns with tradition in challenging non-normativity. In other words, I will attempt to illustrate what I understand my intellectual lineage to be in the construction of this project. I will begin in Ecclesiastes and end in modern queer theology and theory.

Introduction

"I, the Teacher, when king over Israel in Jerusalem, applied my mind to seek and to search out by wisdom all that is done under heaven; it is an unhappy business that God has given to human beings to be busy with. I saw all the deeds that are done under the sun; and see, all is vanity and a chasing after wind» (Eccl 1:12–14). The words of Ecclesiastes describe the existential crisis that plagues the minds of humans who seek meaning in the world and find only wind. In fact, the entire canonical book of Ecclesiastes is filled with individual speculation and striving for meaning. The canonical book of Job is a description of the search for meaning in the midst of suffering in the early Jewish existential tradition. These two books present scriptural examples and descriptions of the constant struggle to know whether or not the individual is able to connect meaning to God, the other, or the self.

Many centuries later, Søren Kierkegaard began to explore the meaning of existence and faith in the midst of futility. In *Concluding Unscientific Postscript to Philosophical Fragments*, Kierkegaard consistently describes the need for a leap of faith or love to overcome the cyclical nature of existential thinking. Faith becomes the way out, but faith is difficult to come by. The leap takes a concentration on both the inward and the outward.[6] In section 125, "The Madman" of *The Gay Science*, Friedrich Nietzsche proclaims,

God is dead. God remains dead. And we have killed him. Yet his shadow still looms. How shall we comfort ourselves, the murderers of all murderers? What was holiest and mightiest of all that the world has yet owned has bled to death under our knives: who will wipe this blood off us? What water is there for us to clean ourselves? What festivals of atonement, what sacred games shall we have to invent? Is not the greatness of this deed too great for us? Must we ourselves not become gods simply to appear worthy of it?[7]

Nietzche's response to Kierkegaard might have been that the task or leap of faith is impossible in the modern age. For Nietzsche,

6. Kierkegaard, *Concluding Unscientific Postscript*, 20–58.
7. Nietzsche, *Gay Science*, 181–82.

life itself was the ultimate revelation of the futility of life and that God was indeed dead.[8] The juxtaposition and struggle between the inward and desire for the outward, however one describes either construct, is foundational to the thought of Kierkegaard and Nietzsche.

The main premise of Martin Buber's *I and Thou* is that humans find meaning in relationships. There are two primary categories of relationships: first, our relationships to objects, and second, our relationship to that which is beyond objects. In order to experience God, one must be connected to the immanent and the transcendent. Buber provides much room for a theology that is connected to the individual and that which is beyond the individual.[9] Along with Buber, Martin Heidegger's *Being and Time* posits that the questioning of the self and the ultimate is at the root of human nature.[10] Throughout his works, Jean-Paul Sartre argues that there is no creator, or thou, and "we are condemned to be free."[11] In *Being and Nothingness*, Sartre argues that being is foundational and nothing else. Buber, Heidegger, and Sartre combine to illustrate the importance of consistently questioning relationships as the essence of being—both the relationship to the self and the relationship or lack thereof to that which is beyond.

Paul Tillich wrote of the courage to be. Being was Tillich's fundamental theological and philosophical construct. For Tillich, there was something supreme about having the courage to exist: "Being can be described as the power of being which resists non-being."[12] Tillich also described God as the God above God.[13] In the theology of Tillich, the being is consistently important, and any experience or connection to a semblance of God happens from the being or the context. In 1961, Gabriel Vahanian published *The Death of God:*

8. Ibid.

9. See the bibliography for further details on Buber's *I and Thou* and other influential works under discussion.

10. Heidegger, *Being and Time*.

11. Sartre, *Existentialism Is a Humanism*, 29.

12. Tillich, *Systematic Theology*, 2:11.

13. Ibid., *Courage to Be*, 188.

The Culture of Our Post-Christian Era. Vahanian proclaimed that God was dead to the modern secular mind and that God needed to be reimagined or resurrected. Vahanian and the other theologians of the Death of God movement created much theological room for theologians to reimagine God. The Death of God movement and the highly contextual ideas of Paul Tillich combined to inspire the creation of liberation theologies from oppressed and marginalized populations that flowed from context.

In *Black Theology and Black Power* and *A Black Theology of Liberation,* James Cone uses his own experiences and the wider experiences of African-Americans to create a theology that posits that God is always most closely described by and connected to the marginalized and the suffering. In these works, Cone pushes the idea that God is black. Later, in *God of the Oppressed,* Cone argues, "What could Karl Barth possibly mean for black students who had come from the cotton fields of Arkansas, Louisiana and Mississippi, seeking to change the structure of their lives in a society that had defined black as non-being?"[14] For Cone, previous constructions of theology and God were unable to speak to the needs of African-Americans, so previous theologies that seemed to leave out the black experience needed to be allowed to die in favor of reconstructing something new. In *A Theology of Liberation: History, Politics, and Salvation,* Gustavo Gutiérrez constructs a theology that speaks of God's dwelling and identification with the poor. The path to the divine liberation of the self comes through the liberation of the poor. Gutiérrez pushes the idea that God is poor. In her *Beyond God the Father: Toward a Philosophy of Women's Liberation,* Mary Daly uses ideas of a divine feminine to reimagine God. For Daly, to say that God is masculine is blasphemous. Through race, class, and gender, Cone, Gutiérrez, and Daly sought to create a God who truly was incarnate in "the least of these." In the coming decades, many other theologians followed suit, daring to believe that liberation would be found in naming their people as the contextual center of God.

14. Cone, *God of the Oppressed,* 3.

In 1968, Anglican priest H. W. Montefiore published a controversial essay entitled "Jesus, the Revelation of God." In this essay, Montefiore argues that Jesus' celibacy could have been due to homosexual leanings and that this might provide further evidence of Jesus' consistent identification with the outcasts and the friendless.[15] Troy Perry published *The Lord Is My Shepherd and He Knows I'm Gay* in 1972. This apologetic text describes Perry's experiences in founding the Universal Fellowship of Metropolitan Community Churches and argues for the full inclusion of the broadly defined gay community. Also in 1972, Howard Wells, pastor of Metropolitan Community Church of New York, wrote a provocative essay entitled "Gay God, Gay Theology." Wells asserts that gay people have a right to God and declares the liberating redeemer to be our "gay God."[16] In 1980, in the seminal *Christianity, Social Tolerance, and Homosexuality: Gay People in Western Europe from the Beginning of the Christian Era to the Fourteenth Century*, John Boswell argues that homophobia was not a part of the early church and that the church should accept gay people for who they are. Montefiore, Perry, Wells, and Boswell all represent the early stages of formulating a queer theology, and those who followed would bring a high level of diversity.

Carter Heyward's *Touching Our Strength: The Erotic as Power and the Love of God*, published in 1989, draws on contextual embodied experience to declare that God not only is present in the romantic relationships of women with each other, but also exists in the very physical sexual acts two women share. In 1990, Robert E. Goss set forth a similar liberation-based theology around gay and lesbian identity in *Jesus Acted Up: A Gay and Lesbian Manifesto*. Though Goss uses queer language in *Jesus Acted Up*, it would not be until the publication of his *Queering Christ: Beyond Jesus Acted Up* in 2002 that Goss would fully explore queer theory within queer theology. Marcella Althaus-Reid took queer theology in a more indecent and systematic direction with the publication of her work *Indecent Theology: Theological Perversions in Sex, Gender*

15. Montefiore, "Jesus, the Revelation," 110.
16. Wells, "Gay God, Gay Theology," 7–8.

and Politics in 2000. The text discusses masturbation, erotic scents, sexual encounters, and much more with the idea that both God and theology are happening in these moments. Althaus-Reid does much to take queer theology in a broader direction through indecency. Patrick Cheng posits that the objective of queer theology is to challenge binaries and boundaries in his 2011 work, *Radical Love*. Through the radical love of God, Cheng argues that all boundaries should be dissolved. Cheng's recent books, *From Sin to Amazing Grace: Queering Christ* (2012) and *Rainbow Theology: Bridging Race, Sexuality, and Spirit* (2013), push further the idea that a God of radical love eliminates boundaries, though Cheng still seems to be very connected to classic language of identity and binaries. For Cheng, love is the unifying force in the universe. From Heyward to Cheng, a broadening of queer theology has taken place. I would like to broaden it further beyond prescribed identities, binaries, and borders to the space of the queer individual.

I have found some of the writings of Chicana lesbian feminist Gloria Anzaldúa to be helpful in describing where I intend to take this project. Anzaldúa writes in *This Bridge We Call Home*,

> Bridges span liminal (threshold) spaces between worlds, spaces I call *nepantla*, a Nahuatl word meaning *tierra entre medio*. Transformations occur in this in-between space, an unstable, unpredictable, precarious, always-in-transition space lacking clear boundaries. *Nepantla es tierra desconocida*, and living in this liminal zone means being in a constant state of displacement—an uncomfortable, even alarming feeling. Most of us dwell in *nepantla* so much of the time it's become a sort of "home." Though this state links us to other ideas, people, and worlds, we feel threatened by these new connections and the change they engender.[17]

I have found the space that Anzaldúa calls *nepantla* to be similar to the space I call queer. I feel like this is the space where all individuals are: somewhere between. The easily labeled normative binaries, dichotomies, and dualisms always fail, but when we dare

17. Anzaldúa, "(Un)natural bridges, (Un)safe spaces," 1.

go to the spaces between, we find the space of transformation, and this is also where we find the self and God. Thus, it is from my own *nepantla*, or queer space, that I write.

The Epiphany of the Queer

I developed a queer hermeneutic based on an understanding that human beings are created to be uniquely queer in the image of a God who is queer and also that resurrection comes through the discovery of the Queer within. I will explore the theology that flows from the use of such a hermeneutic from the pages of Genesis down through the present. Through exploration of the Queer in context, I will illustrate the presence of the Queer in a variety of individuals and contexts. The Bible and human history both reveal the overarching nature of the Queer within and without. I intend to explore the Queer or God in five parts.

The words within the "The Queering" give voice to my mystical experiences of the Queer. Using the developed queer hermeneutic, I intend to explicate moments when I have seen the Queer and encountered the power of God in my own queerness. Visions of love and the Queer have liberated me, and it is important to allow this queer hermeneutical theology to interact with the contextual realities where I discovered it. This space of queerness has served as a launching point for me to discover the God or Queer within myself. The experiences of the Queer within have granted me the ability to create a queer hermeneutical theology. I pray that interacting with the discovery of my queerness will help others discover their own queerness. Upon traversing the meaning of my own discoveries, I intend to bring this queer hermeneutic to consequence on the Scriptures.

Before I describe how I plan to use the queer hermeneutic I have developed, I think it is important to quickly share the reasons I believe a queer theology based on the experiences of the individual is so crucial to our modern context. In the past, fundamentalist and identity-based hermeneutics only functioned if the congregation bought into the premises that the hermeneutics were founded on. I am increasingly encountering younger generations that simply don't buy into the foundational premises. Both the fundamentalist and the identity-based hermeneutic create liberation based on the ability of the individual to belong to a certain group. Within this project, I seek to create a hermeneutic and corresponding theology that liberates based on the individual deciding to fully belong to the God within the self. I think this offers a radically orthodox way forward for the church.

I embarked on this project with the church on my heart and in my head. I simply do not believe that the church can successfully function in the modern age by continuing to consistently create hermeneutical barriers to access and experience. Behold as Jesus stands at the door and knocks. If we dare open the door and usher our churches into the light of all queerness, our churches can be saved. If we remain trembling with fear of all things queer, we will surely die. I believe this project offers a path for us to do something different without compromising who we are. Imagine the beautiful chaos of the Scriptures and Christian practice truly being open to the interpretation of all from their own person. I will demonstrate the use of this queer hermeneutic and theology in three chapters.

In "The Queering of the Old," I will explore the themes of the creating and guiding functions of the Queer found in the Old Testament. I will spend time discovering the Queer within the lives of the characters in prominent stories and passages and analyze the meaning of the results. In the interplay of the stories and passages, I will seek to show the Queer at work and working in the world. This section will push toward a place of discussion of the fullest revelation of God in Jesus or the Queer.

This book's analysis of the Queer within the life of Jesus is entitled, "The Queering of the Queerest." I will spend time in this section analyzing how Jesus embodies the self-actualized queer, or the one who has totally actualized the Queer, or God, within. Through explication and explanation of various moments in the life of Jesus, I will seek to show how the discovery and acting out of the queerness of Jesus embodies Jesus as the Queer. The queerness of God that fully manifests in Jesus makes Jesus God, or the Queer.

This section will seek to illustrate how Jesus shows us the way to finding the God, or Queer, within. The Queer within helps us on the journey to queerer realities.

"The Revolution of the Queer" speaks to the Queer within, or the Spirit of God that is unleashed in all fullness at Pentecost. This third section will seek to analyze ways that the Queer within proceeds to queer or sanctify the world through the individual. From the writings of Luke and Paul to the Revelation of John, I will seek to explicate the queerness of the text. Throughout the New Testament, there are figures that embrace their queerness and others who seem challenged by their finitude to live beyond their constructed, normative selves. This section will illustrate how the Queer functions in the world and pushes us toward a perfected queerness.

The Courage to Be Queer illustrates how God meets us in the epiphany of the Queer. Through the queer interpretation of ancient and modern words coupled with the deep searching of our own souls, we see God calling queers from closets of normative ways of being to step out into the world to unite with other queers and so liberate the self, the other, and the cosmos. Liberation will come for those who dare embrace the Queer. Behold as the Queer stands at the closet door and knocks. I hope these words may inspire many to turn the knob and garner the courage to step out into all queerness so that they might create their own theology from their own epiphany.

1 / The Queering

I CAN REMEMBER THE first time I heard the word "queer." I was eight years old. A bully and her followers on the playground told everyone I was queer. The reasons for the comment were based on the way that I gelled my hair, the way I seemed to know the answers when the teacher asked questions, and the fact that I frequently hung out with a black kid, my best and only friend. In this encounter, the truth of relativity was revealed. The normative constructs of the individual oppressor, and those the individual can convince to follow such constructs, often create that which is accepted as normative or oppressive. My pastor and parents told me I was created in the image of God. I believed them. I realized in this moment of bullying that normativity was being pushed in order to take something from me, something granted by God: my queerness or, better yet, the core of who I am. This is a story of the struggle to discover the will to resist that impulse and instead embrace God's queering. This is an interpretation of my self from a Queer perspective.

Colors

Stark red blood oozed down my face from the gash in my forehead. Everyone was so excited to meet my new baby brother that they accidentally hit me right in the middle of my forehead with the car door in the rush into the hospital. Despite the gash, I excitedly pushed through the stitches and the doctoring to hurry into the room. I put on a nightgown and held Justin. My three-year-old self didn't know what to call what I saw lying there, I just knew there was something unique and different about this child. I think in that moment I began my journey of recognizing and appreciating the queer.

Throughout my childhood, I always loved squinting my eyes to see the kaleidoscope of different colors that came through the brightly colored windows at church. I would contort my head back and forth to see colors dance and pretend that I was in the colors and the colors were in me. Believing that there was something magical going on, I just knew that I was the only person in the world who could see it. I was closest to God in those moments. In the magic and mystery, I knew that I was real and that I mattered. Why do we stop squinting and playing with light? Why do we embrace the normative and shun the queer so easily? I think I was convinced that I needed to grow up.

For a considerable time in my early childhood, my voice sounded like a girl's. When it came out too strong, my parents would tell me not to talk like a baby and that there were consequences for people who sounded like that. I didn't think I sounded like a baby. I thought I sounded like me. From a very early age, I learned that there were normative gender roles I had to fit into and that I needed to adapt to in order to survive. I was led to believe that adapting my voice and life to the expectations of others was a part of growing up. I wish no one had taught me that.

Regardless of the fact that there are similar paintings in churches the world over, I couldn't take my eyes off that old painting of Jesus lovingly embracing a wide diversity of children. Other kids played with the dolls, crayons, and plastic gadgets and gizmos, but I couldn't take my eyes off that painting. From the way everyone close to me talked, Jesus was the one sending most of the world to hell. The painting told a different story. Jesus wanted all the children to come to him. I wanted to run to the Jesus surrounded by children, but I didn't want to have anything to do with the Jesus who was regularly frying people to a crisp. Everyone at church said that these two Jesuses were the same. When I allowed myself to get lost in the painting, I knew better. With every glance,

1 / The Queering

I developed a theology of the painting, and somehow I knew that there was nothing special about a Jesus who destroyed everyone he disagreed with. I was slowly being drawn toward a Jesus who loved everyone. I always wanted to go to him. I did each time I stared at that painting.

"Are you Jeffrey Hood?" the woman asked. I didn't know what to say. By first grade, I knew enough to know that you should be everything except yourself. Being the person God created you to be would only get you disciplined and hinder your success. If you could be like everyone else, then you might have a chance. I remained silent and waited for whatever was next. "Is this him?" she asked my teacher. "Yes. That's Jeffrey Hood."

The woman escorted me down the hall. Due to overcrowding, I was being placed in the classroom of the newly hired first grade teacher, Ms. Ellington. I loved her. Throughout my first day, Ms. Ellington came by my desk to check on me and make sure my day was going OK. I was glad for the switch. I thought Ms. Ellington was much kinder than my first teacher. When I left class, I was excited to tell my mom about the activities of the day. There was some timidity in her response. I didn't know why. When I encountered my grandfather screaming about my new "nigger teacher," I found out.

I didn't know my teacher was black until I was told. Barriers were erected between my teacher and my friends at school based on the color of our skin. I didn't want it to be like this. I resisted the normative racial boundaries. When the time came to study the life of Dr. Martin Luther King Jr., I was all in and recited the last paragraph of the "I Have a Dream" speech to my class. Ms. Ellington made me student of the month. In the juxtaposition of these moments, I knew I was doing something queer and different with Ms. Ellington. I could feel it. I felt like I was being pulled away from the normativity of racism I knew I wanted no part of. Sometimes queerness acts as a life raft to save us from those who love us the most.

Lines

"Line up!" "Who wants to be the line leader?" "Lines keep us safe." "Don't step out of line!" From very early ages, lines become a major part of our lives. We are taught that life is about learning to follow the person in front of us. Our desire to follow the person in front of us is solidified by our desire to one day be the line leader. We are taught that there are dangers to stepping out of line. If we break the line, then we are putting the rest of the line in danger because the authority is distracted when they have to come and correct us in order to secure the line. There are consequences to stepping out of line. Time-outs, letters home, detentions, and other disciplines remind us that we will be punished for such a transgression and keep us from stepping out of line again. The vast majority of people get the lesson early on and stay in line for the rest of their lives. I don't think that this is how God intended it to be. Lines don't keep us safe. Lines keep us normal and therefore sinful. I feel like I have been battling lines my entire life.

Gender lines were enforced very early on in my childhood. People started to look at me funny when my mom took me into public restrooms with her. I got tired of the stares and began to cry when my mom wouldn't let me go to the men's restroom. The pitch of my voice was very high for much of my childhood. Family and friends encouraged me to stop talking like a girl. Through depictions of violence and helplessness, cartoons and movies enforced the idea that women are weak and men are strong. I realized that gender was important to our society and that part of staying in line was staying in your gender line. I felt queerer than that.

"Do you want to go to the toy store?" my grandmother asked. What kind of question is that for a child? I jumped up and off we went. I remember going into the store and found myself bored with the rows upon rows of action figures and baseball cards. I wanted to try something different. So I left my grandmother and went over to play with the dolls for a minute. I found one I really liked and was sitting there pretending like the doll was talking to me when my grandmother came around the corner. "What are you doing? You are a boy. This is embarrassing. Get up! We are getting out of here!" My grandmother's words both startled and offended me. I didn't know what to make of the situation. I do now. In a world where any slight alterations of gender can get you killed, my grandmother was trying to protect me. Unfortunately, she was unable to understand that the Queer God who created me to be queer in the Queer God's image loves me enough to constantly call me to come out of normative lines and play with whatever toy I want to play with.

Something happens as children grow into the many early gender lessons they are taught: the lines we have drawn come to fruition, and children spend years claiming they hate what they perceive to be the gender opposite of them. We organized my second grade class by the genders that were taught to us. There was the Boy's Team and the Girl's Team. From kickball to checkers, the lines were drawn and we stayed in sync to perform our gender roles. As the year went on, tensions built. Finally, the heads of both teams decided that we needed to have one big battle to decide the whether girls or boys were better once and for all. The date was set for the end of the year. Everyone planned feverishly for the playground encounter. When the day came, everyone was in his or her place, and thirty boys and girls went at it in the middle of the playground. There was pulling, pushing, snatching, and grabbing. I still wonder what the teachers on the playground must have thought when they saw it happen. Ultimately, everything was broken up, and we were all left to look at each other with a strange feeling that what had just happened was really dumb. I feel now that what is even dumber is a normative world that teaches us to create and enforce strict gender lines with violence. I think I fought and did all of this to prove that I was a man. I wish someone had simply told me it was OK to be queer.

Sunday schools are often about teaching you the stories of the Bible. Ours existed for one purpose and one purpose only: to get you saved and make sure it stuck. I can remember years of classes filled with the teachers praying for our salvation and teaching us to pray for our own. Whenever anyone prayed the prayer of salvation and got baptized, the class celebrated. For some reason, I resisted much of the charade of it all. I guess I just didn't think it wasn't real for most people and I didn't know why our teachers kept pushing so hard. When I started attending the adult service with my parents, I quickly found out. Hell was on the tongue of every minister who entered the pulpit. The shouts from the pulpit were a constant juxtaposition between anger and grace. We were told that God loves everybody—unless you rejected his advances, and then God was ready to throw you into a fiery burning pit for all eternity. Our God taught us to stay in line at the threat of pain. My home was similar.

Mom and Dad were very young when they had children, and we grew up with them. In both of the homes they grew up in, violence was a way to let out frustration and punish. My mom struggled greatly under the weight of unrealistic expectations and often responded violently and abusively toward her children. I remember living for many years as a child suspended between what I knew was overwhelming love and the threat of violence. I learned to see women as having tremendous power to hurt me. I stayed in line most of the time because I didn't want to be the object of someone else's frustration or someone who needed punishment. I thought that both God and my parents would love me if I stayed in line. Somewhere in my soul—even in the midst of all this—I had an inkling that God had created me to do more than just hold a place in line.

The movie *Dirty Dancing* played on the television. I found the film to be a highly sexual tale of youthful rebellion and discovery. I had never seen anyone move like that. I developed an erection as the colors and people danced across the television screen. I had no idea why my penis had just done that. I was more interested in the screen. My father saw me sitting there and started making jokes about my erection. I did not know what to do. Embarrassment set in, and I ran to my room. I was taught early on that my sexuality was something to be embarrassed about.

Mom was always very suspicious of the sex education offered at school. I was not allowed to attend the earliest classes. So when schoolmates made penis and vagina jokes about what they learned, I had no idea what they were talking about. I felt odd and out of place. When Los Angeles Lakers basketball player Magic Johnson came out as HIV-positive, I had to figure out what was going on. Neither one of my parents would tell me, so I asked one of my older friends. I found out all about sex over a conversation about AIDS. When I told my mom I now knew about sex, she got upset and called my buddy's parents.

Mom wasn't able to keep these conversations about sex away from me for long. My closest cousin had just had a baby. My cousin was not married, and most people in our family did not find out that the baby was multiracial until she was born. Most of my extended family responded very poorly to the news. In the midst of all of this news, I do not remember having any positive thoughts about sex. I thought sex was what got you in trouble, not a queer part of who God created you to be in the first place.

The birth of my multiracial cousin got me thinking. With all of this talk about white and black people, I began to wonder how many people there were in the world who did not fit into the racial dichotomy I was so accustomed to. I began to look around. I realized that ours is a world of many different colors and races. When I inquired about the origins of these racial identities, one of my black teachers told me, "Son, we all have a little bit of everything in us. People matter because they're people, not because of their pigmentation." Right after he said this, I realized he was stepping out of line and that I wanted to step out of line too. Later that day, I told one of our family friends that I thought having the confederate flag on the Georgia state flag was racist. "Are you going to tell me you're a faggot next?" I had no idea what a faggot was. I did not have to wait long to find out.

One of my Sunday school teachers was a kind man who did not fit the fire and brimstone mold. Each Sunday he would gather us in a circle to sing songs about a God of love. He was the sassiest man I had ever known, and I loved him. I never had to worry about him loving me. Slowly, I began to realize that this man was acting out what he thought God was. I found him to be beautiful. Later, he was elected a deacon and placed in many leadership positions in the church. Near the end of elementary school, the metaphorical shit hit the fan. My beloved teacher came out as gay, was kicked out of our church, and moved downtown with his boyfriend. Both of my parents were shocked. When I asked what it meant to be gay, my parents explained that it was two men or two women who have sex with each other. "What's wrong with that?" I asked. "Gay people probably go to hell," one of them sharply retorted. I knew then and there that this was one area I could not step out of line on. I wanted to go to heaven, so I did not question them any further.

Images

Death is an odd part of life. Though death is coming for everyone, no one really knows how to explain it or what to do with it. I realized when a distant cousin died that people will do whatever it takes to explain away an early death. "They didn't take care of themselves." "I bet they were on drugs." "Didn't they have a heart condition?" These types of statements filled the air at my first funeral. Regardless of the cause, I realized when I looked at the casket that death was a normative part of life I was not interested in experiencing. I found it terrifying. I also didn't think there was anything queer about dying. I thought there was something queer about living. Unfortunately, the world I grew up in allowed no room for anyone to be queer.

Weeks after the unexpected death of my distant cousin, someone we had known for many years committed suicide. The revelation that this person committed suicide because they were gay only made me more scared of both death and of my own sexuality. A year or so later, my fears were enforced again. My childhood best friend was found dead after blasting his head off with a shotgun. Even though I didn't know what he meant, I remembered him telling me he liked boys when we were younger. I never questioned the normative belief that these suicides were the natural consequence of people who chose to live in sin, rather than the victims of a society that didn't allow room for people to be queer.

I have never been able to shake the image of my dear friend with a shotgun in his mouth. I think that image of my friend is one of the images that ultimately queered me.

"Do you know beyond a shadow of a doubt where you will spend eternity?" I heard the question over and over again. For the folks in our church, getting saved was not enough. The church wanted everyone to have absolute certainty. Week after week, we talked about the coming rapture of the church and hell. We were always asked to close our eyes, bow our heads, and pray for salvation. I got saved over and over again. Throughout my youth, I suffered from tremendous anxiety concerning Jesus. I was never sure that I believed in the Jesus the church preached about. The anxiety got so bad that I couldn't be alone or sleep. I would freak out when I stumbled on piles of clothes in our house because I just knew that my family had been raptured and I had been left behind. The image of an angry God full of wrath haunted me day and night. I knew that such a God was incapable of loving someone like me.

I was in high school the first time I thought about cutting off my penis. There was a young man at school I thought was interesting, if not outright attractive. I was so afraid of what I felt. What if I was gay? From the eye-gouging language Jesus uses in Mark 9:47, I knew I was better off without a penis than to keep it and burn in hell. The church only made me want to do it more. I felt like life would be better off. Ultimately, I never decided to go through with it. The image of my young adult self staring at my penis and trying to decide whether or not to cut it off still haunts me. I know I am not the only one who has had this experience. I longed for a God who loved me no matter what.

Every word. I have to read every word. If I could read through the Bible in a month, then surely God would love me. I kept reading and reading. I needed to find a wife. What if I wasn't married when I left high school? I can't find anyone who wants to get serious with me right now. I bet my occasional masturbation is the reason I can't find a wife. I know most of the kids at my school are going to hell. In addition to thinking it, I regularly told people they were going to hell. Through brainwashing myself, I started to find the certainty I had always longed for. The normativity felt incredible. I covered up the queer and found the closet to be so comforting.

Certainty

"For those whom he foreknew he also predestined" (Rom 8:29). I recited the phrasing in my head over and over. The life I was living didn't look much like the life Jesus had lived. Auburn University in Auburn, Alabama, is a place where many people talk about Jesus. I joined the crowd. I was in a large, prominent fraternity. I dated attractive women from wealthy families. I made good grades. I had a blast. Since I was chosen, I just knew that God was blessing me. I look back at those years and realize that I was in something of a prison or closet of my own creation.

I started a discernment process and was licensed into the ministry during my junior year of college. After working as a youth minister and preaching regularly for a year, the church I grew up in held an ordination council to determine if I was qualified to be ordained. The council knew I had plans to go to law school before seminary but wanted to ordain me for ministry anyway. I will never forget the first question, "Do you believe in a literal hell?" I faced question after question with the certainty I developed throughout the latter stages of high school and college. When the time came for me to be ordained, many of the people whose teachings had terrified me in earlier years blessed me in my new ministry. The certainty had never felt so good.

Upon graduation, I decided to go to law school. When I arrived, I connected with a local church and started ministering to homeless teenagers. My ministry quickly took over my studies, and I didn't make it to the end of the first semester. I knew what I needed to do. I enrolled in the Southern Baptist Theological Seminary and started studies the following January. Our normative expectations of credentialing creates a world where we don't think about anyone or anything else but the next credential. I thought I had to get more education to be the real-deal Southern Baptist pastor I wanted to be. I don't think Jesus would have left those young people. Maybe Jesus didn't.

The definition of normative is what takes place daily at Southern. From the classrooms to the chapels, professors and instructors teach the same ideas, thoughts, and theology over and over again. By design, there is little deviation from a set understanding of the way things are and are to be. I loved it. For the first time in my life, I could just exist—I didn't have to wrestle deeply with theology and various understandings of God. I was told exactly what to believe, and I did. During this time, I was invited to serve as the pastor of a small country church about an hour north of Southern. I was excited about the opportunity until I found out that the church had female deacons. In my interview, I scolded the church for going against the word of God. Later, I had a female friend who was considering going to seminary to be a pastor. I told her that seminary was not for women. I instructed her, "The Bible says directly that God does not call women to be pastors . . . and to go against the Bible is to sin against God" (I often cited 1 Tim 2:12–14). In all facets of my life, I was the embodiment of normativity.

Professors maintained fidelity to Calvinism through threats and innuendos. I was made to believe that if I cut out any of the doctrine, then I would be in danger of hell. I always carried suspicions that I was on my way to hell and remained in a constant state of anxiety. I was desperate for certainty and did all that I could to try to maintain it. I started to ask questions toward the end of the fall semester. Multiple professors insinuated that I might not be a Christian. Oscillating between certainty and suicide, I spent the winter break in deep thought and returned to school deeply distraught.

Snow and ice were on the grounds of Southern. The buzz of my cell phone startled me, and I jumped up to get it. "Hello?" I answered. "My young friend . . . I'm dying," came the immediate response from my Southern Baptist mentor. Certainty does not allow much room for grief. When I began to softly cry, I rebuked the tears and called my entire person back to the certainty of knowing that God controls all things. On the ride back home, I assured my brain and reminded my heart that God had stricken my mentor with cancer for God's purposes and that I needed to trust that God's glory would come through the cancer. I don't think I ever questioned these conclusions. Certainty can mask a tremendous amount of pain. When I arrived at the house, my mentor's wife ushered me to a back room. We sat and talked for a while. I knew he was disappointed in the certainty I embraced. I felt like he was trying to save me. Fear started to creep in. I had no idea of what was about to happen next.

I stayed awake with my mentor for the last few weeks of his life, and when the time of his death was drawing close, he called me into his bedroom. "I'm gay and I always have been," he offered, then concluded with the following benediction: "Go back to seminary and fight for those who have no voice."

I left shocked and very confused. I knew that my mentor had served as an incarnation of Jesus to me, and I could not figure out how Jesus could be gay. Less than a week later, my beloved mentor died. I met the Queer for the first time in my life and experienced some sort of redemption. These moments were an amazing gift. Leaving certainty behind, I began to venture boldly out of my closet and question the normative world around me. The Queer started to come to me from every direction.

Sanctification

Though I don't believe you can ever really leave God, I quickly retreated from the God I had always known. When you've always been told God is one way, and then all of a sudden you don't believe that anymore, life becomes incredibly disorienting. I felt like I had been bullied at Southern, and I started to push back. Resistance at Southern is always met with screams and condemnations. I didn't know what to do with the pain and struggled to maintain my sanity. I can remember discovering I experienced occasional attraction to men and thinking I was doomed. I was so alone. When I started to come out of the closet, multiple students started coming out of their closets as well. Together, we found love in a hopeless place. The community of the Queer became my refuge.

Upon leaving Southern, I spent a few months finding myself in various jobs and decided to enroll in further graduate work at Emory University. I though the pious, self-proclaimed progressive Methodist, Lutheran, Presbyterian, Baptist, Episcopalian, and other students and clergy would accept me. Most of these folks were not interested in helping someone who had just been at such a conservative school. I didn't have many real friends. In the midst of my struggle, the Queer came to me once more. I found God at intersections of race and sexuality. During my time at Emory, I developed lasting friendships with many people of different race and sexualities. In these spaces of intersectionality, I learned how to be the queer that God created me to be.

Our calling often comes through calls from the past to push into the future. For multiple years, I studied the civil rights movement. I heard the Queer through ministers who risked their lives standing defiantly at normative boundaries of race. The call to be a queer activist and theologian came next. I had no idea what the journey would involve. I simply knew that the path consisted of living into the queer that I was created by God to be.

Traveling abroad nurtures confidence to push into the Queer. When you see queerness being lived out in the face of normativity in other cultures, you gain new strength to be the queer that you are in your own culture. For some time, I grew more and more frustrated with the lack of people around me who were willing to be their own brand of queer. While studying liberation theology in Guatemala, I opened up an online dating account to meet some people. I thought I would never have to tell anyone about it. When I met Emily, I knew I was wrong. People thought we were crazy. We didn't care. We married two months after we met. When you find that you share a queer love with another, you must embrace it with all that you are.

"Wait a little while to have kids," was the normative advice we heard over and over again from both friends and family. We didn't listen. Jeff and Phillip were born ten months after we married.

Not long after their birth, Emily decided to take an opportunity to teach and pursue a PhD in Art Education at the University of North Texas. I thought Texas would be worse than Mississippi. Sometimes I still think it is. Upon arrival, I quickly developed a comfort with living outside the closet.

From blogs to arrests to walks to protests to books to worship to everything that might fall between or beyond, I have lived my life in Texas outside of the closet. I visit Texas' Death Row on a regular basis. I work for Hope for Peace and Justice—the social justice ministry of the Cathedral of Hope United Church of Christ, the largest predominantly LGBT space in the world. I organize and activate people around issues of oppression and marginalization. Through it all, I have discovered that I am most queer when I stand on the side of love. Though I daily wrestle with the pull of the institution or closet to be normal, I walk with God outside the closet.

Born a year and a half ago, Quinley Mandela is our third child. With his birth, I realized my kids need to see us being queer far more than they need to see us being anything else. No one dies and says, "Damn, I wish I could have just been a little more like everyone else." I continue to work to queer my self and the world around me. Recently, Emily gave birth to Lucas and Madeleine. While I don't know what any of my kids will be like, I only know that they were made in the image of the Queer. With the children of the world in mind, I developed this queer hermeneutic so that all who dare open the door of the closet might have a means of exploring the meaning of life, Scripture, and all they encounter that will have the power to transform them from within. In these words of interpretation, may you know the Queer, and may the Queer set you free.[1]

1. The strategy of self-assertion, given the tradition of silencing and erasing the experiences of the marginalized in theology and the church, contributes to breaking through the dominant mode of normativity. My personal journey brings out the queer within me. It is my attempt to be honest and, at the same time, foreground my queer interpretation of the Bible. I would argue that all ministries within the church must also take the non-normative move to question dominant notions of objectivity. All theologies and ministries are contextual.

Hermeneutical Interjection

IN A WORLD DESPERATE for categories and identities to explain everything, mysticism still has the power to lift us beyond to the one true God. The Queer ultimately can only be described from within, for the Queer is unique to each person. We all encounter life from places of tremendous normatized marginalization and oppression. Our hell continues until the normativity is broken and we are able to experience the unique Queer within ourselves. In moments we cannot explain, the Queer somehow meets us in our hell and introduces us to life in the midst of certain death. When we are saved and changed by queerness, we learn to put on new lenses to view all that we come in contact with. I am taking my personal experiences of the Queer and applying them to the chief religious text of my spiritual tradition, but the transformation doesn't end there. There is something integral about those moments when we feel the most queer that give us the power to interpret life queerly. I interpret queerly in hopes that all might experience the liberation that is their own queer hermeneutic.

For most of the people I minister to, there is absolutely nothing queer about the Bible. I felt the same way for a long time. I had a hate relationship with the Bible. I simply had no love for the book. I felt like the Bible was only good for beating me into submission over and over again. In fact, I am surprised to be engaging Scripture at all in this project. Regardless of my frustration with the Bible, there was something that kept drawing me back. I had a suspicion that I would have to go through the Bible in order to reach a deeper queer connection with myself and God.

I don't believe that the Bible is the Queer or absolutely necessary to connect to the Queer. In heaven, I don't believe you will be sitting on the lap of God reading the Bible. Who needs a text of any kind when the culmination of all texts is right in front of you? I just believe the Bible is a part of my past that I have to deal with so it can be helpful to my growth. The Bible is like an abusive parent that I realize I am going to have to figure out how to forgive in order to move forward. In this project, I interact with the text to forgive the violence it has caused even as I look for those passages that can spring me ever closer to myself and to God. I don't believe you can find God in the text. I only believe that you find springs to take you somewhere else. Throughout my reading of the Bible, I am in dialogue with the Queer within and the words in front of me. Through talking to the text and the characters with in it, I experience the spring of the Queer pushing me deeper within and without.

Though this project is based in the liberation of the individual, I argue for an ecclesial approach. I believe that the queer reading and interpretation of the Bible can bring congregations full of queer people together through difference. For the past few decades, the church has relied primarily on fundamentalist and identity-based hermeneutics to bring people together. The problem with these approaches is that they require people to subscribe to or possess certain characteristics to have access to the text or the community. As a result, the church has failed to be a place that is tolerant of queer people or queer interpretations of the Bible, and this must change if the church is going to survive. If the church will allow room for the Queer, the text can be a tremendous means to bring people together. In the unity of queerness, churches can sustain themselves through the beauty of difference. In stark contrast to the older hermeneutics, the queer engagement of the Bible can be the spring to a much deeper knowledge and experience of the self and God for all people.

I am arguing for an alternative vision when it comes to the Bible. In the pages that follow, I will show you where the alternative vision of the Queer took me. I am asking you to follow along and dream about where the Queer is calling you to go. I believe that the text can spring us to all sorts of places and conclusions far beyond the places that traditional hermeneutics could ever allow. The Queer exists somewhere far beyond the Bible. That is where I am trying to go.

2 / The Queering
of the Old

FROM THE INITIAL SIN and violent expulsion of humanity out of Eden to the drowning destruction of the world in the days of Noah to the merciless slaughter of peoples and whole communities throughout its multiple books, I long wondered what to do with so many of the stories of the Old Testament. Even in the pursuit of queerness, I resisted reading or reinterpreting these texts because I found them so unqueer. When I realized that I was letting the normative conclusions of others interpret the stories for me, I started to dream about what these stories might offer if interpreted through my own queer lens.

In daring to queer, I thought about texts that would illustrate and expand our knowledge of origins, the life of the mind, and the struggle for redemption. In the creation story in Genesis, I dreamed of what queer origins might look like. I found the ramblings and wondering of the queer mind to be at the heart of Ecclesiastes. From the flight of Jonah and the queerness of the Ninevites, I learned about the manifestation of chasing queer redemption or queer redemption chasing you. Throughout my reading and interpretation of the texts, the words of Jer 23:24 struck me as I began my journey into the text: "'Do not I fill the heaven and earth?' declares the Lord." In daring to queer, I learned a powerful lesson. If the Queer fills the cosmos, then surely we can find the God who is queer beyond our wildest imaginations throughout these stories about the struggle to know the self and God. The journey to find the Queer in these Old Testament texts is the journey to find the essence of our struggles too.

Origins

The Queer was in the beginning and in the beginning was the Queer. In the abyss there was one being who was different enough from the normative nothingness to push through the nothingness to create somethingness. We call this origin of somethingness God. Others in different languages and cultural contexts have called and call this being something else. Regardless of the call, this one is the queerest or most non-normative actor beyond all time and space. Our attempts to define the Queer will always fall short. In the Queer we begin and have our being.

Beginning and being fill the lines of the first chapter of Genesis. God creates beginning and meaning out of nothing and calls it good. God repeats the task over and over. The center of being is to create meaning out of nothing and call it good. The center of queerness is in the creative task of being and calling it good. God creates out of God's being and calls it good. Being is an active phenomenon that is the beauty of queerness. God is in the being and, in the being, is the Queer. The Queer is God. Our being flows out of the being of the Queer.

There was a conversation that took place in the midst of creation and an early inertia of queerness. The writer of Genesis describes God speaking about creating humans in Gen 1:26. Who was God talking to? I daresay that God is speaking to God's self and pushing the self to the creating task of being once more. "Let us make humankind . . . " (Gen 1:26). The queerness of all of humanity comes next, in what might be the most stunning seven words in all of Scripture: " . . . in our image, according to our likeness" (Gen 1:26). God dares to create and empower humans to create and be queer in being just like God. In the beginning, God is not normative and dares to push through the normative nothingness to be and create being. God creates us to do the same. We emulate God when we dare push through the mundane nothingness of life to be and create being. The Queer creates us to be queer. Queerness pushes back against the normatizing forces that take away life in order to be the creating force of being and life. To be is to live into the image of the creator God and be queer.

God exercises loving guidance over creation and encourages us to do the same. One of the greatest corruptions of queerness is the failure to live into the conclusion of Gen 1:26: "and let them have dominion over the fish of the sea, and over the birds of the air and over the cattle, and over all the wild animals of the earth, and over every creeping thing that creeps upon the earth." For evidence of our failures at dominion, one has to look no further than the agonizing pollution and destruction of our planet. There is a modern normative assumption that dominion means domination and destruction. The Queer exercises dominion by caring about all creation enough to call it good and ask us to protect it. Continued normative failure at dominion will result in the destruction of a queer creation.

The image of God is the most important construct in all of Scripture. The writer of Genesis sees the image as so important that she mentions it twice in 1:27: "So God created humankind in God's image, in the image of God, God created them." What is the image of God, and how should it be understood? Within the person of God there is something that propels God to creatively be and call it good. Being and love are close constructs. God loves by creatively being God's self. Love is a queer construct. Love pushes us to love our self and to love the world around us. There is no construct queerer than being, and the highest form of being is love. The image of God within the human is that which propels us to be and, in being, to creatively love both the self and the world around us. The image of God is the Queer within calling us to be queer and to love both the self and the world. From the earliest of places in Scripture, God is calling us to a space of "I am." The space of "I am" is the courage to connect with the God within and be queer. The one who lives into the Queer, or the image of God within and without, will have the audacity to look at a world of normativity and follow the queer path of God to declare, "I am."

Dualisms, binaries, and dichotomies lead away from the Queer. For those who see gender taking place on a spectrum, there is no more heartbreaking passage in Scripture than the last part of Genesis 1:27: "male and female God created them." The dichotomy of gender at first reading seems to leave out all who would not fit into the binary of a male or female identity. The God who is queer and creates us to be queer pushes us further and deeper in our understanding of gender. The passage says that God created them both male and female, and we should take the words to mean what they say. In each person exists both the male and the female. Our understanding of gender down to how we label our bathrooms and celebrate the birth of children is problematic. If we begin to recognize the diversely gendered queer selves all around us, we will open the door for the Queer God to come out in each other and for the Queer God to come out in our self. We must live into the world that God created past gender binaries and into the Queer. Since God keeps using the pronoun "them" in these passages, maybe "them" is a better way of viewing ourselves with regard to gender.

God encourages "them" to "Be fruitful and multiply, and fill the earth" in Gen 1:28. The Queer grows queerer with the multiplication of queers. The conception and birth of children is a queer phenomenon. To create new life and new queers is to emulate the creative process of a God who dared create humans in God's own queer image. There is grave danger in conceptually leaving out those who choose to reproduce from the Queer. To deny the Queer in them is to deny the reproductive potential in the self. Biological reproduction is not the only form of reproduction. When we dare call humans to step out of the closet and discover the Queer within, we invite them to experience a rebirth from the grip of normativity to a queer place of freedom in creative being. If we are fruitful and loving in our queerness, then we will cause by example and encouragement a multiplication of people who have discovered the Queer within the self. We are called to fill the earth with the creative being that is the queer image of God. The true queer honors and celebrates both biological and spiritual reproduction in order to fill the earth with the Queer.

God repeats the dominion language used in Gen 1:26 in Gen 1:28–30 with one notable exception: the use of the word "subdue," or, in context, "fill the earth and subdue it." The word "subdue" has a connotation of control that can trigger negative thoughts and emotions for many. For the purposes of understanding the Queer God, it might be more helpful to think of the word "subdue" as the means of liberation. We subdue normative constructions in order to liberate our self and others by living into the Queer within. The first individuals subdued or brought liberation to the world around them in order to fulfill the task of living into the Queer within and without. We subdue the normative in order to liberate the Queer. The reason that the cosmos at this point could be called sinless is because creation was subdued to liberation and the liberated Queer was continuously cultivated everywhere. This passage illustrates that humanity is an intimate partner in the creation and continuation of the Queer here on earth.

The final verses of the first creation account in Genesis speak of God calling all of creation good and taking a rest. These passages are perplexing in that they leave one to wonder if God gets tired and decides to stretch out for a nap. The meaning seems to be much deeper than exhaustion. God speaks to us in this space to let us know that sometimes the queerest thing to do is to just be. God pauses in the queerness to soak in the goodness. We are called to emulate this practice. There are times when we must simply stop for a good rest to revel in our queerness.

The second creation account describes the creation of humans in a different way. In Gen 2:7, God forms man from "the dust of the ground, and breathed into his nostrils the breath of life; and man became a living thing." If we couple the first creation story with the second, we have to wonder what kind of man was this. The first creation account says that God created humans to be male and female. Was this a genderless person with regard to the way that we understand gender? How could this first person be male or female when neither construct existed yet? Maybe God just knows the queerness and beauty of each individual. Could it be that our creation and ordering of gender binaries has caused the destruction of the queer image of God in every human? The Christian project of turning the first person into the manliest man that ever existed has desecrated the queerness of the first people and has consistently pushed to destroy the recognition of the queerness of all of us. God breathed a unique breath of life into the nostrils of the first person and also breathes a queer breath of life into all of us. Will we dare live into the breath?

The beauty of the first people's home in the garden of Eden is described in overwhelming measure in Gen 2, yet there is something lurking in the background. There is this odd tree of knowledge of good and evil, and God says, "but of the tree of the knowledge of good and evil you shall not eat, for in the day that you eat of it you shall die" (Gen 2:17). I have always wondered why God put that tree there in the first place. Why put a tree in the garden if you know that all it is going to be good for is tempting the occupants? This tree reminds me of one of my teachers growing up telling our Baptist youth group about the dangers of masturbation and remarking at the end, "Don't try this at home." Give me a break. Come on, God . . . What's up with the tree? I think the answer lies in the queer. Risk is always deeply connected with the Queer. God takes an enormous risk in creating humanity and continues to take the enormous risk of loving us. The Queer always takes risks and pushes us into dangerous spaces to discover and live into the ground of being. Perhaps the most loving thing that God did in creating the garden was to put that tree in the middle of it and challenge the inhabitant not to eat of it. In the temptation to be something else, perhaps we are given direction and encouragement to discover what it means to be queer.

God decides to make the first person a "partner." God tries out all of the animals with the first person, and none of them work as a partner. One has to wonder, what did it mean for the first person to try out the animals? So God takes out one of the first person's ribs and creates the second person. Though the Scripture calls the second person "woman," we have to return to the first creation story to figure out what we are really talking about. God created them both male and female. So the rib actually created a person that is of the same constitution as the first person: both male and female. The first queer relationship happens when these two come together, become partners, get naked, and are not ashamed. In the words of Gen 2:23, the beauty and freedom of two queer bodies coming together, partnering, and becoming bone of each other's bone and flesh of each other's flesh cannot be denied. The borderless ways that God describes gender in the first creation account pushes us to a place of dreaming beyond our dichotomies and binaries.

There was a serpent that slipped into the garden. Since the gender of the first two people has become rather ambiguous and blurred, we do not know whether the serpent approaches the first or second person in Gen 3:1. How could we? To the blind, normative eye of the serpent, both queers would be indistinguishable in their queerness. When the serpent comes and tempts one of the first individuals to eat of the tree of knowledge of good and evil, the serpent becomes the great expositor of the story. The person goes over all the rules God gave about the tree, and the serpent replies in part, "You will not die" (Gen 3:4). In some ways the serpent is telling the truth; the serpent knows the grace of God and that the death the person will experience if they eat of the tree will be one of denial of the Queer within, not necessarily an immediate physical death. The person eats, and their partner eats of the tree too. The consequences are immediate.

Theologies, constructions, or explanations of the human experience must account for the origin of evil. In order to find the way of redemption, we must speak to the pain that all experience. So what happened at the tree of the knowledge of good and evil? I think it tremendously shortsighted to claim that this is simply an act of disobedience against God. Something happened in the person who took the first bite—an internal decision produced an external response. To consistently speak of outward actions is to deny the war that rages within every person between the normative and the queer. The normative is always constructed based on the desire to be something other than what God has created each person to be: queer. The serpent promises, "you will be like God" (Gen 3:5). The failure of the person who took the first bite was not simply an act of outward disobedience to some outward God. Their failure was a denial of the self, or a denial of the God within. The first bite meant that the first person wanted to be made like some outward God and failed to realize that the path to God takes place in the journey to find the Queer or God within. There can be no queer when our efforts are centered on trying to be like anyone else. The first sin is always in the first bite, thought, or step to deny the queer that God has created us to be. We can call the normative sinful because it is the evil construction that pull us away from the Queer.

To journey back a half-sentence, in the first part of Gen 3:5 the serpent tells the person who took the first bite, "God knows that when you eat of it your eyes will be opened." The prevailing strategy of evil against queerness is to convince those whose eyes are open that they are blind. The serpent succeeded at convincing the first biter that they were blind and their eyes could be opened wider. When we live into our queerness, there is always the temptation be like everyone else to be accepted. We struggle to exist as the queer God created us to be because there are those around us trying to convince us that we are simply blind to how wide our eyes could be opened. The normative entities don't realize that we only appear blind to them because we are too focused on the queer to gaze upon normatizing evils. The primary response to the evil of normativity must be to keep reminding ourselves that our eyes are wide open to the Queer, that God created us to be queer, and that there is no need to be given sight by anyone else. The cry against evil must be "Our eyes are already open."

The second bite into the fruit came when the person who took the first bite gave a piece to their partner. How often do we accept the pieces of normativity that people offer us? The first offer came from the serpent, and the person who took the first bite passed it on. At each point in this economy of evil, the self and God within is denied to chase after the normative offer of another. The normative is sinful primarily because God calls us to be the queer individuals God has created us to be and not spend our lives desiring to be somebody or something else. The serpent passed evil along by causing the first people to think they needed something more than the Queer inside them. Misery loves company, and there is always the temptation to pass along normativity when we are not feeling quite so queer. This is the reason that evil continues. If we want evil to stop, we must stop the cycle and simply be the queers God has created us to be.

The consequence of eating the fruit is an immediate attack on the body. Genesis 3:7 recounts, "Then the eyes of both were opened, and they knew that they were naked; and they sewed fig leaves together and made loincloths for themselves." This opening of eyes was really a blinding. The sight that the serpent promised was really blindness to the queerness of the self. The immediate attack on the body made the first people ashamed of their bodies, and they felt the need to cover them up. When we fully connect to the queer or God within, we are able to develop a comfort with and care for our bodies that the normative constructs of the world cannot take away. Believing the lies of the attack on the body is often the first consequence of denying the Queer within and being blinded by normativity.

God came to visit after the great denial of the Queer within that took place with the first few bites. Genesis 3:8 describes the scene thusly, "the man and his wife hid themselves from the presence of God among the trees of the garden." When we deny the Queer, we try to hide from the Queer, but we don't realize that we cannot hide from the God that made us queer in the first place. We can try to cover up and hide all that we want to, but God is never going to stop seeking us and will eventually find us. When we begin to deny the Queer within, God often comes to remind us. The presence of the Queer is always the force that stands against our desire to stay in normatizing spaces. Indeed, God showed up to say, "Where are you?" (Gen 3:9). God didn't ask out of confusion about where they were. God asked as a means of soliciting admission of where they where. We have to admit to our self and God that we have traveled far from the queer God created us to be before we can begin the journey back to that perfect place of creation.

The person replies to God in Gen 3:10 with "I heard the sound of you in the garden, and I was afraid, because I was naked; and I hid myself." The first people had never experienced fear before. Fear arrives at the denial of the queerness within. When we chase normative constructions, we are always afraid that we do not meet the normative expectations of others. We are especially afraid of God when we know that we have denied the Queer within. In our denial, we arrive at a place where we do not know what to do except to hide. We hide the very core of who we are from the world and assume that no one will notice. The history of humanity is littered with the creation of closets. We think we are naked, and so we hide. The problem is that we do not realize that our naked self is amongst the most beautifully queer constructs in all of creation. The Queer does not have to hide.

"Who told you that you were naked?" God inquires (Gen 3:11). This is an important question for anyone who desires to live queerly and be free. The answer to the question is the source of our shame. Who told you that you are naked? Who told you that you are ugly? Who told you that you are insignificant and without value? Who told you . . . ? The answer to the question also grants us a path to freedom. For if we can identify the cause of our shame, then we can also illuminate the path to freedom. There is a deeper question. Are we going to believe God or are we going to believe the ones who have lied to us? We can be who and what God has created us to be or we can choose to be what those who have lied to us and laid out categories for us to follow. The choice is ours. Will we believe the Queer, or will we believe the liars who call us elsewhere?

One person blames the other for the crime of denying the self: "The other made me do it." Our othering keeps us from the task of freeing the self. The longer we blame others for our normality, the less likely we are to discover the freedom of the Queer. The first person blames the other person. The other person blames the serpent. Blame is the name of the game, and no one stops to seek the mercy of God. We spend so much time on our explanations of what is going on and why we are who we are that often we don't see the liberation of God standing in front of us.

There is a naming that happens after the fall, and the struggle for power commences. Genesis 2:20 states, "The man named his wife Eve." The man is quick to assert his power over the woman. Make no mistake, sexism and genderism are a result of the fall. God offers us a path to a different dimension where labels and identities are less important. When we travel the path of the Queer, we become the unique image of God beyond identity that we were created to be. Categories and identities fall away, and we are invited back to be our self, existing in peaceful community with the self and each other.

Recreations of the creation event are unfortunately colored by the categories and identities that would have blinded the author, but God seems to leave a remnant of truth that can guide us to greater understanding of who God is and who we are. The story of Eden is the denial of being. We must get the Queer back if we are ever to be truly queer. If we have the courage to depart the normative closest, we will probably spend our entire lives trying to get back to the place of perfection we are from, but I believe the queerness that Eden offers is the place of being worth traveling to.

The Mind

Growing up in a small town in the Deep South was not kind to a young seeker who questioned freely, and so the seeker moved to the big city to enjoy more room to explore. Looking to drown out the pain of previous years, the young seeker invested in all sorts of distractions. The joint temptation of drugs and sex became a regular indulgence. When this didn't work, the seeker threw their life into accumulating money. When that didn't work, the seeker invested in knowledge. Over and over again the young seeker cycled through avenues of exploration in attempts to arrive at meaning. Ultimately, the young seeker paused and decided to collect their thoughts. The book of Ecclesiastes is something similar to what might have resulted from such a pause. The narrator of the book is named Kohelet, and his mission is to discover meaning or being.

The search is in the text and its conclusion is in this being—in being who we are, we discover the Queer.

"Vanity of vanities! All is vanity," moans Kohelet in Eccl 1:2. The young seeker has tried to find meaning in everything, and nothing has provided meaning. Mania has filled the seeker's life as they have grasped at anything and still found nothing worth holding onto. Kohelet has carried a supreme belief that he will be able to discover something in the normalities of life that will give life significance. There has been dead end after dead end, and yet still nothing. The fatalism in Kohelet's search is not lost on the modern person. Those who seek to discover meaning by following and doing the normative things everybody else does consistently arrive at dead ends and are left to moan, "vanity of vanities! All is vanity."

The external search for novelty and excitement that plagued Kohelet is the same search that plagues us. How often do we stop to speak the words of Eccl 1:9, "there is nothing new under the sun"? The search for newness is the search for something external to derive meaning from. The seeker works, enjoys pleasure, and pushes for the latest new thing precisely because the seeker lacks the power or capability to just be. There is nothing new under the sun because the newness we need is within. The queer image God has created bubbles beneath the surface, waiting for us to return even as we suppress it and try to find newness somewhere else. Kohlelet dodges the Queer in exclaiming, "The people of long ago are not remembered, nor will there be any remembrance of people yet to come by those who come after them" (Eccl 1:11). There are dangerous memories that lurk beneath the human experience—dangerous memories of being queer in a faraway past. The problem in the search for meaning is that we lose sight of the Queer within that comes to us in being. We look to the past and see so much failure. We forget that we are the only ones who can push past vanity to being. The original memories of the Queer lead us there.

Time is a false way of talking about meaning. Meaning is found in time, but ultimately there is a component of meaning that transcends time. Being is timeless and eternal just like the Queer. Being is beyond time and space but reaches within it. Meaning

without being is fruitless. The queer can stand with Kohelet and declare in the words of Eccl 3:11, "*God* has made everything suitable
for its time; moreover *God* has put a sense of past and future into
their minds, yet they cannot find out what God has done from the
beginning to the end."[1] There is a time to be born and a time to die,
but the Queer or being is beyond such things. Everything happens
in a suitable time, but God uses the sense of past and future to call
the individual into the eternal place of being queer. The closer the
words "being" and "queer" are used together, the more we realize
that they often carry the same meaning. The normativities of time
and space threaten to steal our soul if we search for meaning only
in them, but when we cling to the being or queerness that is beyond
time and space, we begin to gain the immortality of the Queer.

Oppression and marginalization stifle queerness. When we
are constricted, inhibited, or prohibited from being who we are by
the fear and consequences created by others, God comes to us and
sits with us until we embrace our liberation. Kohelet misses God's
presence in Ecclesiastes: "Again I saw all the oppressions that are
practiced under the sun. Look, the tears of the oppressed—with
no one to comfort them! On the side of their oppressors there
was power- with no one to comfort them" (Eccl 4:1). Kohelet falls
into the trap of not examining how his own actions and thoughts
have oppressed others. We know that Kohelet was a man of great
means, and we are left to wonder whether Kohelet's pontifications
are taking up his time and inhibiting him from being an actor
for the liberation of others. Those familiar with academia and attempts at higher learning understand the temptation of Kohelet's
musings about oppression. I think the words of Eccl 4:5 apply:
"Fools fold their hands and consume their own flesh." The fools
fold their hands and talk about oppression as they consume their
own flesh. Perhaps the talk is part of the oppression. Perhaps our
tendency to talk about oppression keeps us from being the Queer
that is needed to liberate. We are all oppressed when we allow that
which is normal to control our responses to oppression. We are

---

1. I often substitute and italicize the word "God" in place of gender-
specific pronouns referencing the Godhead.

all liberated when we reject the normalcy of marginalization and oppression and instead accept that only the Queer within and without can liberate the cosmos. It begins with us.

Religious spaces are tricky places for the Queer. In Kohelet's musings in Eccl 4:9–10 we find the longings of the queer: "Two are better than one, because they have a good reward for their soul. For if they fall, one will lift up the other; but woe to one who is alone and falls and does not have anyone to help. Again, if two lie together, they keep warm; but how can one keep warm alone?" Humans share a basic need for community. The queer knows it is better to not be alone, but the problem is that the queer is consistently tossed out of our churches. This ritual of oppression has happened so many times that the queer is left to wonder if the institution of the church can ever be a home. There are so many falls and so many times when no one is there to pick up the queer, which leaves the queer wondering if anyone will ever be there to bring them in from the cold. When two are united in being, they are warmed. When God joins us and we quit trying to seek acceptance from places that are never going to value the queer, we become strangely warm, for we know that another is there. The queer must stop looking to the institution of the church to find warmth and look to God, whose flame will never be extinguished. The queer can only warm in the presence of the one who provides the fuel, and that fuel comes from the Queer within.

Dangerous memories creep back in when queer folk think about the church. Throughout time and space, the church has been one of the world's great weapons for destroying the queer, silencing the masses, and imprisoning the spirits of billions. Often, God has used the church to liberate in spite of the normative institutions that claim to be the church. Kohelet speaks directly to those who have found the church to be a harsh place in Eccl 5:1, saying, "Guard your steps when you go into the house of God." Take a few wrong steps, and you might just stumble into the den of evil. These spaces look like churches, but they are death factories for all things queer. Normativity is thrust at the queer at every step and threatens to stifle the very queer image of God within, but Kohelet gives us advice in the

49

middle of Eccl 5:1: "to draw near to listen is better than the sacrifice offered by fools." In other words, you better listen to what the folks at the church are saying to figure out whether or not they are fools. Fools wallow in their own evil normativity with no regard to the damage they inflict on the message of the Queer in the process. The fool hates the queer, for the queer brings the only true wisdom of being. Stay away from the fools, "for they do not know how to keep from doing evil" (Eccl 5:1). The fool comes to steal, kill, and destroy, but the Queer comes to bring the life to being and the being to life. Be on guard against spaces that are run by fools, which is most of our churches, for they cannot handle the Queer.

Is it better to be pushed toward dreams or to listen to the incessant talking of fools? The question of Eccl 5:3 rings true in the lives of all. The queer image of God that is within us pushes us toward the immortality of being. Immortality is always the stuff that dreams are made of. When we connect with dreams, our minds and spirits travel back to that place called Eden we remember from long ago, for it was there that we knew what it meant to be queer. In Eden, we knew what it meant to just be. The Queer within us calls us back, and we have some sense that we were born for more than the incessant talk of fools. The dreams call to us daily, begging us not to follow the normative commands of fools. Shall we carry the cares of dreams we might not ever fully grasp or follow the normative commands of fools over and over? The cares of dreams that come with being queer are light in comparison to the dark stifling weight of life with no meaning.

"Better is the sight of the eyes than the wondering of desire; this is also vanity and chasing after the wind," declares Kohelet (Eccl 6:9). There is a difference between desires and dreams. Desire pushes us into the pleasures of the flesh and tricks us into believing that the fulfillment of desires is what constitutes dreams. Kohelet rightfully believes that desires can only lead to chasing after the wind. In this conclusion, Kohelet fails to see the power of dreaming about what once was in the garden of Eden and what could be again. When we dream of the queerness of love, we dream of God. Unlike our desires, which as flow aimlessly as the wind, God is in our dreams. When we pursue the non-normative dreams that God has given us, we walk queerly with God.

There is much talk in our world, and there always has been. When we humans cannot accept our inner queerness, the temptation is to spend all of our time seeking to create boundaries for others. We have to define what is going on. We have to name and identify others. We participate in such activities with the hope that somehow our definitions will not be used against us. The problem is that we know how much we define and talk about everyone else, so we are suspicious that they are defining and talking about us. In listening, we discover this negative perception of our self, and with such a discovery comes greater insecurity about living queerly. Kohelet speaks of this phenomenon in Eccl 7:21–22, saying, "Do not give heed to everything that people say, or you may hear your servant cursing you; your heart knows that many times you have yourself cursed others." So how do we keep from getting caught in this mind trap of talk and fear, which will inevitably keep us from God? We pray that God will help us to understand that the normativities we place on others are the same normativities being placed on us. We pray that God will help us to live outside the cycle of normativity and invest in expressing our true selves from the trap of insecurity and the desire to be something other than what God has created us to be. We can free ourselves from casting normativities on others and on ourselves. We can be queer if we can only quit all the talk and all the listening and just be.

The normative world believes it has found the solutions to all that could possibly afflict it. We have created rules, identities, borders, and boundaries for everything. We believe that being normal keeps us safe. The enemy of God in the modern world is not the unruly spaces, but rather the safe ones. We are taught that it is both safe and proper to get an education, work hard, retire, and die. If there is any deviation from such a plan, one is called a deviant. The normative path leads to worldly respect but not to the answers we humans are looking for—the gnawing questions of meaning always remain. The path of least resistance does not lead us to a queer God or self, and such a path is therefore not of God or of our truest self. Kohelet was correct in the last part of Eccl 8:8: "nor does wickedness deliver those who practice it." The wicked is not what you think. The wicked is all the safe things that keep you from the Queer within.

God comes to us in being. There is nothing that we have to do except be. Kohelet speaks of the temptation to always try to do something more beyond being, saying, "Again I saw that under the sun the race is not to the swift, nor the battle to the strong, nor bread to the wise, nor riches to the intelligent, nor favor to the skillful; but time and chance happen to them all" (Eccl 9:11–12). God does not call us to be swift. God does not call us to be strong. God does not call us to be intelligent. God does not call us to be skillful. Time and chance can quickly destroy our abilities in all of these things. God calls us to be. When we cling to the Queer within and without, the world, no matter how calamitous, cannot take our queerness away. When times of disaster come, we shall not be moved if we cling to and plant ourselves in the Queer who is greater than the normative calamites around us, the Queer who is higher than any potential destruction, and the Queer who is the great rock of ages firmly planted in our being from the start of creation.

God created our bodies to be treasured and valued as beautiful and magical throughout our lives. Since the loss of perfect queerness and the onset of normativity in Eden, humans have consistently longed for and romanticized the days of their youth. There is tremendous folly in failing to accept the Queer, and a manifestation of such folly is hallucinating about and yearning for former years. Kohelet presents a stunning rebuke of such thinking: "Even those who live many years should rejoice in them all" (Eccl 11:8). It is normative to yearn for our youth. It is not normative to embrace the Queer at every stage of life. The queer person remembers that "the days of darkness will be many" (Eccl 11:8) but lives on in a refusal to be distracted from being. Kohelet knows that "all that comes is vanity" (Eccl 11:8), yet all that is simply is. The queer has to answer the temptation to long for former years with a bold declaration of queerness and the is-ness of being.

The musing and wandering of Kohelet's mind mirrors our own musing and wandering. We know the vanity of this life and the many normativities it consistently offers us, but we struggle to grab hold of and cling to the queerness that comes from being connected to God. The mind and soul are tempted to race toward distraction after distraction, keeping us from being queer. We search for an end to all of this madness. There is an end to normativity. After all has been heard and pondered, Kohelet reminds us that there is a queer place that once was where we can return home to again: "Fear God and keep the commandments; for that is the whole duty of everyone" (Eccl 12:13). When we try to be something other than what God created us to be, we are lying. God is truth, and the truth always comes out. We are to fear God only when we wrap ourselves in normativity and fail to embrace God. The Queer has created us to be queer and therefore commands us to return from our wayward normativities. God calls us back to that queer space that is Eden so that we might be fully queer once more. The duty of everyone is to keep the commandment of being queer and to create a world that is queered by love. The life of the mind and soul takes us in many directions, but we must remember that the mind and soul will be restless until we rest in the Queer.

Chasing

The credibility of the story of Jonah does not depend on the edibility of its protagonist. Whether the reader finds this story credible depends on the reader's ability to queer their mind and place themself in Jonah's shoes. We all have our Ninevahs. The tale of Jonah is not about a man who lived thousands of years ago; it is a tale about us.

God spoke. The story begins with a word from God. People throughout history have claimed that they have heard a word from God. You always have to be careful when someone tells you that God has spoken. Sometimes people are crazy, and yet sometimes people are truly more attuned to God than anyone else. The proof seems to be in the doing more than in the hearing. The doing is what seems to prove that Jonah heard something. God told Jonah to go to Ninevah, and he declined. The evidence of an encounter is found in the difficulty of what God requested.

When people claim to hear God speak, God often says what people want to hear. God always seems to call people to higher-paying jobs. God always seems to promise better health. God makes requests of people that seem to be exactly what the person who claims to have heard from God wants. While it is impossible to verify all claims of God speaking, we are able to gather a fairly good idea of whether or not God is speaking based on the difficulty and desirability of God's request in the midst of our comfort with normativity. Queerness is a difficult place to travel toward. If queerness were easy, then we would all still be enjoying the graces of Eden. We can rest assured that the word of God is contained in what Jonah claimed God said, because God tells Jonah to go and be a part of the queering of Ninevah. In the Queer is truth, and the truth of this tale is that Jonah is called to go. The great energy the Ninevites exhibit in favor of normativity is to be transformed into great energy for queerness. Jonah is called to come out to Ninevah.

Jonah didn't want to have anything to do with the Queer. Jonah wanted to continue to live life away from God and not have to worry about awakening the Queer in anyone. Tarshish was the closet where Jonah thought he could hide, but the truth of the matter is that God was calling Jonah to come out as queer to the people in Ninevah, and anything short of that was already closeted. Closets are made for the fearful, not for the free. Sometimes we have to go to great lengths to stay in the closet. Jonah got on board a ship and hid below in order to try and stay in his closet. Jonah thought that he could hide from the Queer, but he failed to realize that we can never hide from our creator. The Queer is always inside us and will always be revealed.

The mighty storm raged and the winds blew. The ship that was Jonah's closet began to break apart. Everyone near Jonah's closet thought they were going down with him. We hide from the Queer, and we expect those who know we are hiding to keep our secret. The problem is that when the mighty storms hit and the closet starts to break apart, everyone is running for their lives. When lives are on the line, you cannot expect people to protect your closet at the expense of their lives. Jonah slept through all of this and probably thought that he could sleep his way to saving his closet. Many think that they will be able to sleep through the mighty storms of revolution and come out of the closet when there is no danger. When we stay closeted, we think we are protecting ourselves when really we are sleeping through everyone else's demise. The captain of the ship was not having it, and we should hope that the captains of our ships don't either: "What are you doing sound asleep? Get up, call on your god! Perhaps the god will spare us a thought so that we do not perish" (Jonah 1:6). The captain wants Jonah's god to spare them a thought, when really it is Jonah who hasn't cared about anyone onboard enough to give them a thought. In a world where selfishness is the norm, it is queer to love others, and Jonah's actions from the closet of the norm have proven very unqueer thus far in our tale.

Despite the calamity, Jonah still tried to stay in the closet. The sailors decided to hold a lottery to figure out what the hell is going on. The lot fell on Jonah. The closet door was flung open, and the outing began. As the winds howled and the rain poured, the sailors demanded answers. Jonah poured fear upon fear when he told them that he was running from God. The sailors knew that no one can simply outrun God. Pouring fear upon fear in the midst of normativity is a great pastime of those who insist on running from the Queer. Normative people run from storm to storm and closet to closet thinking that they will outrun the outrunable.

Throughout our lives, we find ourselves in the boat with the storms raging around us—will we give into despair, or will we simply accept God's call on our lives to be queer? The sailors are trying to figure out what to do with the dead weight. Truly, the sailors want to be free, but they don't want to have to cut Jonah loose. Queer communities often face this problem. Do we hold on to dead weight, or do we give the person to God? Like the sailors, we often hold on tightly to the deadest and most closeted amongst us. The sailors kept rowing to keep from having to toss Jonah out, but you can't out-row the Queer. Ultimately, Jonah asks to be thrown overboard, and the sailors have to oblige in order to save their own lives. There are times when we have to give people to God in order to save the rest of the community. The queerest act we can partake in is letting go and trusting the Queer. The storm stopped raging.

Jonah is thrust into a time of testing. Talk about rock bottom—the belly of a fish becomes Jonah's home for three days and three nights. The belly of the fish is also the middle of the tale. Between the closet and the coming out of the queer lies this space of between. In the space of between, we travelers must wrestle with God's desire to save us from the closet of normativity and our desire to stay in the perceived safety of the closet. Jonah was torn in that space of between for a few days, and then he started to pray. We must be careful about what we pray for in that space of between. Shall we pray for the Queer to be manifested, or shall we retreat back to the closet in fear? The Queer called, and after a time between, Jonah answered.

The queer prayer of Jonah is long but simple: "Deliverance belongs to the Lord!" (Jonah 2:9). The struggle to embrace the Queer, move past the space between, and truly be free of the closet is heard in every syllable. Jonah wants to be free and prays with an expectation that God is going to provide. Queerness is trusting that God will set us free when we dare to let go of the normative things we think we can manipulate and control. The acidic vileness of the belly of the fish is where Jonah first finds the beauty of the Queer. If we let go of the normativity of control, deliverance comes from God in places where we least expect to find it. Prayer summons the great liberator. Our queer, expectant embrace of the one who created freedom sets us on a path to free others. The fish puked Jonah up. Past the closet and the space between, Jonah was now queer and ready to queer others.

On the beach, Jonah feasted on his queerness. After some delay, God came to Jonah a second time and instructed him, "Get up, go to Ninevah, that great city, and proclaim to it the message that I tell you" (Jonah 3:2). Jonah listened. Upon arrival at Ninevah, Jonah looked around and instructed the folks to all embrace the

Queer within. To Jonah's surprise, the people of Nineveh repented and embraced queerness with their whole beings. From the King of Nineveh down, everyone repented and came out. God met the Ninevites as they exited their closets of normativty and embraced them in love. Jonah was pissed.

One nasty side effect of developing queerness is the constant normative temptation to believe that your queerness is somehow better than the queerness of everyone else. Jonah did not want the Ninevites to embrace their queerness. Jonah wanted to stay in that space of queerness alone. When we become selfish and aggrandizing with our queerness, we give in to the normative temptations of selfishness and pride. Queer celebrates queer and does not grow angry as it finds renewed expression.

Jonah couldn't take seeing his enemies become queer. Rather than see the Ninevites uncloseted, Jonah wanted to die. Feverishly, Jonah prayed with great expectation that the Ninevites would be destroyed in their normativity. Jonah even traveled outside the city and set up a booth so that he could have a front-row seat for the destruction of Ninevah. How often do we hate those who leave their closets and become queer? We want to see them fail. In our hateful normativity, we are disgusted by their freedom. There are tabloids and other forms of media created to make a spectacle of people being destroyed in their queerness. We are a people so tempted by normative selfishness that we don't know how to act when people embrace the queerness of their true selves. Outside the city, Jonah waited on the destruction of Nineveh. The problem was that Nineveh was now the queer one, and Jonah was the one who had backslidden into normativity.

There are times when God allows closets to come and tempt us to go back in. Shade came from a plant that grew up next to Jonah. This plant provided much safety for Jonah, and then God allowed a worm to eat it away. The safety of the closet was no more. The sun came out, and Jonah wanted to die. God rebukes Jonah for his selfishness. The closet is often a selfish space where we think we are safe and don't care what happens to anyone else. The problem is that death comes quickly in the closet. Death of the soul and spirit leads quickly to the death of the physical being. Queerness is the only thing that can revive the one perishing in the closet. Jonah curses God for not protecting his closet of safety. God points to Nineveh. "Should I not be concerned about Nineveh, that great city, in which there are more than a hundred and twenty thousand persons who do not know their right hand from their left, and also many animals?" (Jonah 4:11). God is pushing Jonah toward love and concern for a place where people didn't know anything about queerness a few days before. The Ninevites have confused their dichotomies and found salvation in such confusion. Queerness' freedom comes from refusing to be defined or bound by normal standards.

The blurring of right and left is of the utmost importance in the book of Jonah's final triumph, but the last four words of questioning push this queer triumph even further. The blurring of right and left is of the utmost importance, but the final four words of questioning push the queer triumph even further: "and also many animals?" (Jonah 4:11). God's concern for Nineveh extends beyond the human occupants of the city to those we typically consider subhuman, or at least denigrate by calling them lesser species. So why does God mention the animals? Is God like the Buddhists in their concern for all sentient beings? Could it be that queerness extends beyond the human to all of creation? The answer is that God's concern extended to the whole of creation found in Nineveh, and our concern must extend to the whole of creation we meet. The Queer loves and cherishes all life. We would do well to follow the Queer.

The Old Queered

Some might still find the words contained in the Old Testament too heavy with normativity and not worth carrying into our modern age. To those I must declare, there is nothing more normative than forgetting where you come from and failing to work to redeem it. Our origins are what give us a platform from which to launch ourselves into wider queerness and also grant us a space from which to sacrifice so as to be redeemed. The queerest one, called Jesus the Christ, understood the importance of the principle nature of origins. One cannot study Jesus the Christ without carrying old words and finding the healing revelation of God in them and in spite of them. We cannot be a people queered and redeemed without old words. So let us carry them inward and onward into our beautiful queer future.

3 / The Queering of the Queerest

"I MET JESUS ON a cold, dark, stormy road . . . " I don't know why people think their testimonies have to be so dramatic. I doubt there are enough "cold, dark, stormy roads" to account for all the testimonies that include them. Regardless, I think it is important to teach consistently that Jesus comes to us in the queer situations and intersectionalities that we inhabit. I am tired of narrow interpretations of these stories that leave little room for wideness in the incarnated love of God. Even in the ancient time, Jesus was queer. Why have we dequeered these stories? Where is the wildness in our interpretations? I believe that queerness and wildness flows and compounds from the queerness of the God within us. Does Jesus grow queerer still? I believe so.

The Temple and the Years Thereafter

The road to Jerusalem was full for the festival of the Passover. Hordes of people and animals moved in lockstep to be a part of the particularly holy occasion. Whether walking or riding, a young Jesus traveled too. We do not know what filled the mind of Jesus. Was Jesus thinking about seeing old friends? Was Jesus thinking about worshipping God? Was Jesus thinking about the party in Jerusalem? To provide answers to any of these questions is nothing more than speculation, but I have to believe that Jesus was not planning for this to be the time when he would come out to his family and religious community. Sometimes things just happen serendipitously or as God' surprise.

Coming out is part of the queer experience. For the queer, there are always those moments of standing up and realizing that the words you speak or the thoughts you let play out are the queerest things that anyone around you has ever heard or thought of. Jesus was not unlike most twelve-year-olds. The trip to Jerusalem was a time of mental, spiritual, and bodily discovery. For the first few days after his arrival, Jesus experienced and engaged the space. Then, the Queer started moving and shaking. Mary and Joseph left Jerusalem and thought Jesus had too. When they couldn't find him, Mary and Joseph returned and searched Jerusalem for three days.

Jesus' coming out story is similar to many. After you come out, people often have difficulty placing you or finding you. Most of the time, this inability to find the Queer is due to people's inability to think like the Queer or see the Queer. Mary and Joseph were not thinking like Jesus and had tremendous difficulty finding him. When the two parents finally stumbled on their child, they discovered Jesus in all his queerness. The religious teachers were amazed that a child could teach like this. People had never heard or experienced anything like this before. When his parents questioned him in their deep anxiety, Jesus responded, "Why were you searching for me?" (Luke 2:49). The answer in the form of a question speaks to the queer experience. Those who seek to find the Queer fail to see that the Queer is ultimately within. The desperate search of the heart and mind is futile until the heart and mind rests queerly in God. True growth comes from soaking in the Queer: "Jesus increased in wisdom and in years, and in divine and human favor" (Luke 2:52). Where?

One of the queerest mysteries about the queerest person to ever live comes from an inability to determine where Jesus was during his silent years. From age twelve to thirty, little is known of Jesus. Various speculations and revelations have placed Jesus everywhere from Judea to Britain to Egypt to India to even the Americas during this period. The truth is that there is very little evidence to support any of these conclusions. We simply do not know where Jesus was during this time. Maybe the queerest response to silent reflection is reverence. Maybe in those silent years Jesus was learning to be Jesus. Don't we all need that time? Reverence for silent incubation of the Queer must always be maintained. Noise is normative, of course. Those who make much noise with few words are probably the queerest. Jesus proves such a hypothesis.

The Righteous Queer Anger

The normative reaction to injustice is apathy. Most ignore injustice and would prefer to continue simply living their lives without interruption. One cannot be close to the heart of God and be comfortable watching people suffer. Jesus lived close to the heart of God and was uncomfortable when he walked into the temple. Discomfort is a queer response to injustice that should quickly lead to a righteous anger.

Throughout the temple, people were selling animals and changing money. On the surface, these actions seem simple enough. I am sure people had been selling animals and changing money at the temple for many years before Jesus arrived. People were just accustomed to the merchants. Injustice becomes normative when people step back and declare something is righteous because it is the way things have always been. Queerness causes us to look deeper. Jesus realized that the merchants were creating a financial barrier to the worship of God. Poor people couldn't buy the animals for sale, and we can safely assume that the best exchange rates did not go to those with the least. In the midst of an oppressive financial barrier to the worship of God, Jesus got angry.

People often falsely assume that there is nothing positive about anger. The person who lives queerly should always be angered by injustice. Jesus makes a whip of chords and drives out all the animals. Jesus turns over the moneychangers' tables. Screaming, "Take these things out of here!" Jesus demands an end to injustice (John 2:16). The righteous queers amongst us will capture the anger of Jesus and start driving out all tools of injustice. The normative will be the ones who run the other way.

The Second Birth

Fear keeps us from coming out in the daylight. Sometimes we have to search the night before we can find the day. There is truth to be found in the darkness that can push us toward the light. Nicodemus came searching for truth. Full of grace, Jesus opened the door and let the closeted man in. The conversation between the free Jesus and the closeted Nicodemus began with an affirmation.

Conversations between the out and closeted often begin with an affirmation. It is as if the closeted person thinks they have to affirm the value of the out person they are talking to. What they don't understand is that God has already set the person free, and there is no need for further affirmation. Spaces full of people who are truly queer have no use for affirming or reconciling ministries. There is a queer celebration of life and birth always going on. The mistake of Nicodemus is to hold back and think that one can be queer merely by affirming the queerness in somebody else. Queerness begins with a personal affirmation, and this embrace of what is within you is what flings open the closet door and sets you free.

In John 3:3, Jesus says one must be "born from above." God creates us uniquely queer in our first birth, and somehow as life drags on, we suppress the Queer within. When someone points out that we are not queer and living dishonestly, the conversation can often turn testy. Our entire being is aware that there is something untapped or missing in our lives. The Queer calls us to be free. Nicodemus knows that he is closeted and is flustered by it all, asking, "How can anyone be born after having grown old? Can one enter a second time into the mother's womb and be born?" (John 3:4). Queer conversations often get stuck in the physical processes. Nicodemus is stuck in the physical and refuses to see that queerness is about freeing the whole person. Jesus replies, "What is born of flesh is flesh and what is born of the Spirit is spirit" (John 3:6). This is a spiritual, queer birth that frees the entire person. When the queer rebirth happens, it is unexplainable: "The wind blows where it chooses, and you hear the sound of it, but you do not know where it comes from or where it goes. So it is with everyone who is born of the Spirit" (John 3:8). When queerness calls a person out of the closet of normativity, the person cannot be easily defined or tracked. No one knows how they got out or where they are going next. We are simply left to do one of two things: we can accept or reject the calling of the Queer to freedom. Nicodemus still couldn't figure it out.

Perhaps the most famous verse in all of Christian Scripture reminds us that God loves the world and God sent God's child to earth so that the world might know the path to salvation (John 3:16). Queerness comes through following the Queer. Nicodemus was not ready. Nicodemus loved his status, position, and normativity more then he loved the freedom of queerness that Jesus offered him. In John 3:19, Jesus spoke of the choice between darkness and light. Do we choose the closet, where life dies, or do we choose to step into the light of freedom and honesty with our self and others? Queerness arrives when we embrace the light, and it develops into fruition when we live into our second birth. To stay in the closet that is self-destruction is to deny the Queer and slowly die from the inside out. Normativity is what keeps the door of the closet locked. The queerness of a second birth is the key to open the door to the light. Those who have stepped into the light are called to stand with Jesus in concern for others trapped in the closet of normativity and declare, in the words of John 3:7, "You must be born again!"

The Well

The thirsty met at wells in Jesus' day. Lying down next to the well, Jesus demanded a cup of water from a Samaritan woman who had just walked up. Those whose sight is short might dismiss this as a patriarchal demand and dismiss it before ever arriving at the next verse. This is a queer encounter to be defined by Jesus' liberation of those stuck behind identity borders and boundaries. Surprised, the woman replies, "How is it that you, a Jew, ask a drink of me, a woman of Samaria?" (John 4:9). Jews and Samaritans didn't even speak, and yet Jesus spoke to her. To speak into destructive vacuums of injustice is to emulate the Queer. Jesus would not be silent. The woman could not understand. *Why would anyone talk to me?* Jesus started rambling about living water. Courageously, the thirsty woman kept asking for more information. In seeking living water came an answer of universal, eternal proportions: "those who drink of the water that I will give them will never be thirsty" (John 4:14).

We live our lives thirsty. We sip violently at the waters of normativity over and over again to no avail. Our thirst is not quenched, and we grow bitter about the parchedness that has invaded our hearts and souls. Jesus offers an answer that is queerer than anything the Samaritan woman has ever heard—living water that causes the thirst to finally go away. The water causes the drinker to truly live. The water causes the drinker to truly be. The water puts the drinker in direct contact with the Queer within and without. Shall we stop and tarry with the Queer at the well? Eternal life speaks to the quality of life one experiences both now and after death. Jesus connects queerness with the possibility of living queerly now and in the life beyond. The Queer at the well offers a queer beverage for those who are queer enough to stop for a drink.

The Samaritan woman had traveled from man to man for years to find something to validate her and give her life meaning. Ever the great liberationist, Jesus argues that the spirit and truth of God is all that she is being offered and all that she will ever need. At this moment of beauty and consequence, you can almost hear the great queers of time and space filling the heavens and chanting, "Chug! Chug! Chug!" The woman tries to explain what is going on, and in the explanation, stumbles on the answer. Jesus comes out once more as the Queer. The revelation carries with it a reminder that coming out is a constant state for the Queer in our world of normativity. With each movement of speech or thought, the world questions the Queer. How can anyone live as a unique individual created in the image of God? Truly being queer is unfathomable to most people, whose lives are largely overtaken by the normativities of this world. The revelation of Jesus stands in direct opposition to the unfathomability perpetuated by normality and declares, "I am he" (John 4:26). In Jesus' affirmation of the self is the Queer. In our affirmation of our own selves is the Queer.

Throughout the accounts of Jesus' life, moment after moment arises when the lack of queerness or sanctification in Jesus' disciples or followers becomes painfully obvious. Jesus is having this beautiful moment with the Samaritan woman when the disciples walked up "astonished" (John 4:27). The Queer who breaks all the borders and boundaries we create is astonishing and often leaves people speechless. If people stare or are astonished by you, remember that they stared and were astonished by the queerest of them all too. The Samaritan woman didn't pay the disciples any mind. For the first time in her life, the woman was free to avert the stares and simply be the Queer that God created her to be. The Queer is contagious, and the Samaritan woman ran into the city to share what had happened to her. In shock and disbelief, the woman shouted out, "He cannot be the Messiah, can he?" (John 4:29).

Folks who shun queerness are most often concerned with the temporal and mundane. Unable to fully understand the liberation that has just happened, the disciples are concerned about food. Jesus is concerned about the harvest. The mission of the Queer is to set others free. Those who truly embrace their queerness cannot help but want to liberate others. The Samaritan woman wanted her community to be free. There is nothing queer about being concerned only with your own liberation while the community around you remains enslaved. The woman works for the liberation of all, and "many Samaritans from the city believed in him because of the woman's testimony" (John 4:39). The liberation of one causes others to believe that the Queer is the liberator of all.

The Adulterous Woman

Jesus consistently dares to push into moments of incredible clarity and make them exceedingly confusing. In the confusion is the Queer. Without confusion, we are left to explanation. When we have explained faith we have killed it, for truly faith is unexplainable, and so is the Queer. Jesus was in the temple to teach what it looks like to be a confused follower of the Queer. The Pharisees—the day's masters of clarity—approached him with a legal matter. There was a woman who had been caught in the act of adultery, and the law stated that she needed to be stoned. Clarity reigned before things turned very queer.

There is no question that the woman was terrified. Trembling, she stood before Jesus. The Pharisees described her crime and questioned Jesus through deep stares, asking, "Now what do you say?" (John 8:5). Clarity demands answers, and queerness offers blurred replies. The normative world looks to each individual and demands that they identify themselves and then act within that identity. There must be clarity! There must be boundaries and borders to keep us ordered and under control! There must be identity so that there will not be any confusion about who or what we truly are! There must be a plea! The Queer takes all of these musts and transforms them into a confusing amalgamation of queer. When the Pharisees demand that Jesus condemn the woman, he starts writing in the dirt. Liberation is often found in the dirt.

The dust was not settled, and Jesus started to write. While we don't know exactly what Jesus was writing, we do know that it pushed the accusers to keep questioning. I have always believed that Jesus was writing the names of the Pharisees' forbidden lovers in the dirt. Whether or not such a conclusion is true, it does bring up an interesting question: Where was the man? The identities, borders, and boundaries the Pharisees constructed and accepted in their own minds allowed them to exact a punishment on the woman with no evidence of any thought or action toward the crimes of the man. The misogyny of the moment should not be lost on anyone. Jesus gets involved in this injustice against this woman because he believes her, in all her queernesss, to have the utmost value in the eyes of God. We must get involved in situations of injustice because we believe in the inherent queerness and worth of every person.

Our collective desire to execute those we believe have performed violent acts against us is normative. The queerer place from which to react against violence is a place of grace and forgiveness.

Grace and forgiveness challenge the normativity of a world bent on vengeance. When we allow violence to be met with violence, we are contributing to a normative, destructive cycle that does nothing but oppress and marginalize. It is important to point out that adultery is a violent act and that the woman and man involved committed crimes against their families and others, but death is not the punishment for this crime or any other. Reconciliation and forgiveness cannot take place when someone is dead. The penalty of death denies the power of the Queer to transform the world. Jesus illustrates that to deny the power of the Queer to transform the world is to deny the Queer.

"Let anyone among you who is without sin be the first to throw a stone," Jesus responded strongly to the adulterous woman's eager executioners in John 8:7. The stone test brought the Pharisees to a place of consciousness before the attack. Jesus looked them in the eye and demanded an answer. There was no answer to be given. No one has the right to kill the body or the soul of anyone. The Queer pushes us to be queerer in a world of violence. "Put down your stones!" Jesus calls. The stone test is always the love test. The queerest among us will always be the ones standing with empty hands and open hearts.

One by one, the accusers packed up their accusations and walked away. The light of the Queer reveals the destructiveness of normativity and rebukes all who cling to the lie of process before people. Jesus looks to the woman and declares, "Go your way, and from now on do not sin again" (John 8:11). To ask the woman not to sin again is to reveal that the adultery was indeed a sin. It is a mistake to assume that queerness grants room to engage in sex without limits. Selfishness is a normative construct that encourages us to do what feels good. Unfortunately, what feels good is not necessarily the queerest thing to do. Sex is abusive and hurtful when engaged in without love. Perhaps a queer sexual ethic should be: sex and love should always go together. Regardless of the terms, the actions of the couple caught in adultery hurt people and were wrong. To respond queerly to situations of pain and hurt is to respond with grace. Stones are not graceful. Love is graceful. Love is the presence of the Queer and is the only queer guide forward.

The Light

The adulterous woman was set free. Evil and shame were banished through the light of truth and love. Everyone looked to Jesus to say something, and then he "spoke to them, saying, 'I am the light of the world. Whoever follows me will never walk in darkness but will have the light of life'" (John 8:12). The truth is the light, and the light is the truth. The Queer is the light, and the Queer is the truth. The very presence of Jesus changed a situation from darkness to light. There had to be something tremendously queer about this man.

For Jesus to say that he is the walking and breathing light of the world is for Jesus to stand in a world of normativity and declare himself queerer than all creation. The queer difference that Jesus made in the life of the adulterous woman is recreated over and over throughout the gospel narratives and beyond. Jesus is the light of the world because Jesus sets people free. Jesus made the difference because Jesus was and is different or queer.

Like a blast of the brightest light possible, Jesus dispels darkness. Queerness functions as a blast of bright light into a dark closet of normativity. The Queer illuminates all that is normative, and that which is normative cannot stay in the presence of the Queer. The light destroys the closet. Those who follow the way of Jesus will be queer and will not walk in normativity. Those who embrace the queerness endowed to them by their creator will not walk in darkness but will "have the light of life" (John 8:12). The light of life is the Queer.

The Dead Man

The love and ministry of Jesus is extended to everyone. So why did Mary and Martha approach Jesus saying, "he whom you love is ill"

(John 11:3)? There is something queer or outside of the normative about the love that Jesus had for Lazarus. Though Jesus loved him queerly, Jesus waited two days to go to his bedside. There were many in Judea who wanted to kill Jesus, but Jesus waited for another reason. The queerest moments come about when we wait for the magic of the Queer.

"Lazarus is dead" (John 11:14). In spite of the danger of the detractors, Jesus demonstrates that queerness always pushes toward death, not away from it. The disciples thought they were going to die. Queer courage fuels the journey. Two miles from the house, Martha runs out to meet Jesus and makes a queer statement: "I know that God will give you whatever you ask" (John 11:22). Later, after seeing the tremendous grief of the gathered, "Jesus began to weep" (John 11:35). The tears represent the pain associated with queerness when it encounters such a normative construct as death. Jesus pushes into the situation and arrives at Lazarus' tomb. "Lazarus, come out!" Jesus shouts (John 11:43). Lazarus was unbound, and the lovers intimately embraced. The beauty of such queer love will always be suspect in a world of normative. When Caiphas, the high priest, heard about all of this, he declared that Jesus must die for the nation to "gather into one the dispersed children of God" (John 11:51–52). Even Caiphas believed that the Queer could bring people together. Jesus knew that the Queer does bring people together through the queer conquering of death. Lazarus is one of a mighty wave of death-conquering feats of queerness that still continue.

The Declaration

Jesus swung his head back and declared, "I am the way, and the truth, and the life. No one comes to the Father except through me. If you know me, you will know my father also. From now on you do know him and have seen him" (John 14:6–7). We know God is queer because Jesus is queer. Non-normativity is what makes Jesus special. If Jesus was normative just like everyone else, then we would not still be talking about him. There is something magical in the difference that is this queerness.

Jesus is the way. Jesus shows us that queerness in a world of normativity allows us to follow him and be the difference needed to make a difference. The path to a Queer God is through a queer person who shows us how to live and believe queerly. To take the path of unbelief and despair is normative. Jesus shows us a higher way. Jesus shows us the truth. There are those who want to believe that power is the truth. Jesus queerly shows us that the sacrifice of love is the truth. Everything that is not queer is a lie. We must push into the truth of the Queer within to find life that is honest. Jesus is the life. If we embrace the Queer, we will have life. Jesus is the perfect incarnation of the Queer. No one comes to God except through queerness. Jesus is the incarnation of queerness. No one comes to God except through the Queer, for the Queer is God. Jesus made a difference by showing us all the way to be different.

The Judgment

The judgment of man was all around Jesus. Queers are always judged from all sides. There were Pharisees and others who felt the teaching of Jesus was not judgmental enough. We can be sure that there were others who thought Jesus was too strict. People judged Jesus based on their varying perspectives and often on a sliding scale. To set the record straight, Jesus explains what the real judgment will be.

In Matt 25, those who know God are those who embrace close encounters with the least among us. The normativity of our moment is that we live in a world that teaches us to race past the least. The message of Jesus is to stop and queerly soak for a while with God. Too often, we get in a hurry and miss the queerness that can make us whole.

The means to feast were controlled by a small minority of the population while the rest of the population starved. Jesus places his queer body alongside those who are starving. Those who fill their mouths at the expense of others perpetuate the normative evil of greed. It is normative to aspire to be the one whose plate is full, but it is queer to aspire be the one whose plate is empty. The true followers of the Queer will be those who place their lives alongside the hungry.

There was a drought of compassion in Jesus' day. People were thirsty, and most of the population just watched them burn. When you are thirsty, it is normative to drink up all of your water and not care about anyone else's thirst. Jesus says that he resides with those who are thirsty. The queer among us will learn to thirst.

People regularly traveled across borders in Jesus' day. Kindness and welcoming spaces were difficult to come by. There were those who died out in the elements. Normativity encourages us to keep our doors closed, install an alarm system, and be afraid of the stranger. Jesus invites us to welcome in those we might find strange. When we give our lives to the queer at our door, we become queer. The Queer comes into us in the strangeness of the stranger, and in such a God is our salvation.

Jesus is nude. When Jesus reveals his genitals, is there a penis, or a vagina, or something between, or maybe even something altogether different? Does Jesus shave Jesus' pubic hair? Are there any piercings? Are you the first person to see Jesus' genitals in this way? Jesus welcomes such questions when he declares his nudity and expresses solidarity with those who have no clothes. The poor are exposed, and we are called to expose ourselves too. Queerness is standing naked in the midst of a world of empty clothes.

The isolation units of Jesus' day were places in the streets where diseased people lay and cried out for help. Isolation was the normative response to all sickness. Jesus declares his love for and solidarity with the sick during a time of stinking open sores and devastating diseases. Those who want to follow God are told that they have to bring in and care for those the world isolates. One cannot be queer and continue to isolate anyone, whether it is the self or the other.

Those who thought they were going to find the Son of God coming on the clouds missed Jesus behind the bars of the prison. It is normative to believe that people in prison have no dignity or worth. Jesus calls us to a queerer space of engagement so directly that we must be willing to be with those the world has shunned. The doors of the prison slam behind you, and you know that you are with the Queer.

"'Lord, when was it that we saw you hungry or thirsty or a stranger or naked or sick or in prison, and did not take care of you?' Then he will answer them, 'Truly I tell you, just as you did not do it to one of the least of these, you did not do it unto me'" (Matt 25:44–45). The judgment of God comes from a queer dimension where the least are the most. Those who pursue God will seek to live in that queer dimension. The queers are the ones who become so incarnated with the least that it is impossible to tell who is the least and who is not. In the midst of this land of spiritual poverty, the queers will be called children of God.

The Garden

Queerness can lead us to dark places of uncertainty where often feel the queer path ahead is too much. The oppression of normativity swirls round and round, threatening to engulf us with each step. We do not know what to say or do. People around us have been inspired by our queerness and are looking to us for instructions on what to do next. Jesus responds, "Sit here while I go over there and pray" (Matt 26:36) or "Sit here while I pray" (Mark 14:32). There is a crisis brewing, and Jesus tells the disciples to sit. Like the disciples, we want to respond queerly to the overwhelming injustices of our time, and Jesus says to sit. We protest and want to do something. Jesus points us in a direction indicating that in the being is the doing. We must sit for a second and learn how to be queer before we do anything queerly. Sometimes in the sitting is the doing.

Jesus senses that great harm is rapidly approaching. Jesus knows that an injustice is about to take place. In the midst of such grave concern, Jesus does not go out and seek to stop what is coming. Jesus stops to pray. The queerest act in the face of injustice is prayer. Everyone believes that it is the responsibility of the offended party to fight back and bring the fight to the oppressor.

People look at you as if you are crazy when you don't prepare to fight back. As the hour of violence was coming for Jesus, he told us what to do: pray. Despite all the violent normative possibilities of what might come next, the queer thing to do is to stop and pray.

The space of prayer is a difficult one. Recognizing the violent range of possibilities, we want to avoid whatever might come next. Jesus is deeply grieved and struggling to remain queer. Looking at the disciples, Jesus begs, "stay awake with me" (Matt 26:38). We do not think we can go on unless we have people around us. We do not think we can go on unless people approve of what we are doing. We want people to acknowledge our queerness. While others fall asleep in the midst of our agony to remain queer, we must remember that we are never alone because the Queer is always within us.

Mixing dirt and tears, Jesus writhed on the ground, desperately trying to figure out a way around the rapidly approaching oppression of normative violence. The last temptation of the Christ is to give up the Queer. In spite of tremendous pressure, Jesus holds onto the Queer and declares, "not my will, but yours be done" (Luke 22:42). In the embrace of the Queer, Jesus places his very body into the struggle for queerness in our world. Jesus decided to go all the way. When we decide to go all the way, celestial beings begin to walk with us and assist us as we move forward: "An angel from heaven appeared to him and strengthened him" (Luke 22:43). I don't know what the angel looked like or said, but I know that the presence of the angel made Jesus feel the presence of the Queer more strongly. Incarnating the perfect, queer love of God into our world was always his mission, and he would not be moved. The journey of the Queer leads to life through death, and even as blood dripped to the ground from his agonized body, Jesus stayed in the garden.

Throughout the agony and temptation, Jesus returns intermittently to check on the disciples. At one point, amidst the roar of their snoring, Jesus turns to Peter and questions, "Could you men not keep watch with me for one hour?" (Luke 22:40). The answer for the disciples was a firm "no," and the answer for so many disciples now is a firm "no." There was a queer revolution of love going on, and the disciples were asleep. Throughout the centuries, disciples have slept through queer revolutions of love. Presently, many disciples are sleeping through queer revolutions of love going on all around us. In the midst of our present revolution, Jesus makes the same request now as he did then: "stay awake with me" (Matt 26:38). The question remains, "For what?" Jesus says, "Watch and pray so that you will not fall into temptation. The spirit is willing, but the flesh is weak" (Matt 22:41). Jesus knows the temptation to leave the queer path of resistance to normativity and stop pursuing the Queer. Even though they keep falling asleep, Jesus wants his disciples to be a part of the revolution. Unfortunately, not everyone can arrive for the revolution at the same time. Sometimes we need to follow those who have gone before us for a way before we find our own Queer within. The disciples were not ready to go the way of the Queer. Jesus was and still is.

The time had arrived for Jesus to be delivered into the hands of normative guys not all that different from many religious leaders today. The disciples had not yet experienced an awakening. Only Jesus was ready for what was coming next. There is a tremendous lesson to be learned in this moment. If you are not ready to embrace your queerness, then follow those who have. There was little time for the disciples between the decision to get up and the violent arrival of the great tempters of normativity. This is what every day looks like for those who are following the path of the Queer. There is always little time between the decision to get up and the violent arrival of the great temptations of normativity. The disciple named Judas ran up to plant a kiss on Jesus, who replied, "Friend, do what you are here to do" (Matt 26:50). Even in the midst of a tremendous betrayal Jesus knew would lead to death, he called the perpetrator "friend," and there is nothing normative about that. In a world where vengeance and violence is normative, the Queer leads us to call our enemies and betrayers "friend." The queerest part of you is the part that can conjure up love in the midst of hate. Queerness held firm, and the hands, fists, and swords started flying.

Knowing they were not ready to drink from the queer cup of consequence, Jesus requests that the disciples be let go in John 18:8. Falling victim to the normativity of violence, Peter is not ready to go and slices off the ear of Malchus, a servant of the high priest. Jesus screams, "Put your sword away!" (John 18:11). In these moments of unimaginable struggle and oppression, the normativity of violence is rebuked for all time and space with just a few words. Jesus declares, "for all who take the sword will perish by the sword" (Matt 26:52). Weapons don't have anything to do with queerness. Those who truly follow the Queer resist such violent measures and peacefully follow the one who the Queer sent to the cross.

Jesus declares, "all of this has taken place, so that the Scriptures of the prophets may be fulfilled" and "Then all the disciples deserted him and fled" (Matt 26:56). Everyone wants to know the way of God until they find out that it leads to death. Everyone wants to hear a word from God until such a word requires their own life. Everyone wants to seek God until God leads them to a place they do not want to go. The word of God was being proclaimed, the Scriptures were being fulfilled, and the disciples of Jesus took off. We are in no position to judge. We do the same thing. We must resist the normative urgency to flee in the face of oppression. Queerness requires that we stand, and when we have nothing left within us except the Queer, we must still stand. Queerness requires that we give our lives to the battle against normativity even unto death. Queerness requires that we follow the word of God even when it does not make normative sense and we do not want to. The assembled actors of normativity carried Jesus away. There was no fight, because Jesus was and is the Queer.

The garden is the climax of the human experience. It is in the midst of the tears, blood, and agony, Jesus decides that the queerest way to live—and the way to follow the God who is the Queer—is to give his life for love. There are doubts and struggles. There are opportunities to fight back. Jesus will have none of it. Jesus is committed to the way of the Queer: the way of selfless, unconditional love. If Jesus had stopped, he would not have been the embodiment of the Queer. Jesus did not stop, and this is why we can still call him the Queer.

The Supper and the Suicide

After handing out some broken bread he declared to be his body, Jesus took the cup of wine and said, "Drink from it, all of you; for this is my blood of the covenant, which is poured out for many for the forgiveness of sins. I tell you, I will never again drink of this fruit of the vine until that day when I drink it new with you in my Father's kingdom" (Matt 26:26–29). Jesus asks everyone to drink. Jesus uses the word "all" and alludes to a coming realm where all things will be restored. Judas had just left the room. In speaking of the coming restoration, Jesus' mind could not have been too far from the restoration of his betrayer.

The authorities condemned Jesus. Condemnation is a normative construct. Judas felt condemned by everyone. Judas was heartbroken and tried to make the situation right by returning the thirty pieces of silver. "I have sinned by betraying innocent blood," he said (Matt 27:4). The authorities would have none of it. Judas ran out and hung himself. It is important to remember that these events happened not long after Jesus instituted the meal. Before his death, Judas made a move toward God through repentance. God is about grace, not condemnation. I believe that Jesus met Judas after his death with the cup and the bread. Even if Judas denied the cup and bread the first time, the Queer found Judas and was able to make him whole. Relentless love in the midst of continuous betrayal and condemnation is what makes the Queer the Queer.

The Question on the Crucifix

The weight of the world proved heavy. Jesus hung on the cross for many hours. Torture was an understatement. In the midst of the pain, the Son of God cried out, "My God, My God, why have you forsaken me?" (Matt 27:46). This might be the queerest moment on the cross. Jesus shunned the idea that faith must be without doubt and embraced the darkness of the hour. In these courageous moments, Jesus is God. For as we know, God was and is Queer in the darkness. When we sit in the darkness expressing doubt and yet clinging to faith, we become the Queer in the darkness.

Commencing the Rescue

> "All authority in heaven and on earth has been given to me. Go therefore and make disciples of all nations, baptizing them in the name of the Father and of the Son and of the Holy Spirit, and teaching them to obey everything that I have commanded you. And remember, I am with you always, to the end of the age."
>
> —Matt 28:18–20

Jesus has all authority because he is the queerest of them all. Through his very life, we are shown the path of the Queer. Jesus tells us to go and make queers of the world. When we dare follow the way of the Queer and simply be queer, we give others the courage to be the queer individual the Queer is leading them to be. The Queer works through the Queer in each of us to unite us in our queerness. This is the very rescue mission of God—to save a planet with fleeting memories of when we were queer. Though normativity tempts us at every turn and the darkness surrounds us, we can come together and be the queer light of the world. Remaining with us until the end of the age, the great Queer of all queers promises to lead us into the fruition of all queerness. By being who we were created to be, we begin to queer the world.

4 / The Revolution
of the Queer

WIND IS SEEN OR heard when it makes contact with objects. The Queer functions similarly. Movement and noise come from contact. Reaching out to the world, the Queer moves to create queerness, and the contact creates visibility and noise. These visions and noises create the symphonic soundtrack of the incarnation of a queer world. Unique individuals join together in community to lead the queering. Pentecost is just the beginning of the stunning revelation of what happens when the Queer gets loose.

Pentecost and Peter's Stifling Sermon

There is danger in not thinking about the Jesus movement with a queer sense of broadness. In creating borders around what the Jesus movement is or isn't, people are left out. On the day of Pentecost, Acts 2:1 says, "they were gathered together in one place." From the previous chapter, we can assume that this "they" consists of at least the eleven apostles. So is the church made up of only apostles? The day of Pentecost is presented as a different day than when all of the apostles are gathered. So is it possible that the "they" is broader than who we might think or even wish were present? The Queer often brings other unexpected queers to the table. What if the "they" who walked up included people of a variety of religions, races, classes, and genders? Maybe Pentecost was so queer that the writer was unable to list the wild diversity of people God touched in their own context.

Unity can be a forgotten value when one focuses on uplifting the queerness of every individual. The Pentecost crowd gathered together in one place. This group did not have to be of one doctrine or understanding to know that there was something coming and that they wanted to be a part of it. Those who follow the Queer know something is about to happen, and they gather together because they want to be a part of it. Unity in difference or queerness ushers in the eruption.

"And suddenly from heaven . . . " (Acts 2:2). Something happened, and it happened quickly. The accompanying description of what happened might reveal what the group was doing in their waiting. The writer describes something coming out of heaven. How would anyone know what heaven was unless they had been taught? Did the something come out of the sky, or did it come from another place entirely? Where is this heaven that the writer speaks of? Perhaps God was there teaching the gathered what to look for and how to know when it has come upon us? Queerness is an individual process that begins with allowing the Queer within each of us teach us how to describe and where to look for the eruption.

The sound came out of heaven. What do the sounds from heaven sound like? We can assume that the noise was not the stereotypical melodies of harps. The writer says that it was "like the rush of a violent wind" (Acts 2:2). The sounds of heavy metal music mixed with the sound of a freight train were probably closer to the melodies coming out of heaven in this context. The sound was violent, and violent sounds are unnerving and dislodging. God came out to the world once more as the Queer at Pentecost. To those who were the keepers of the many evils of normativity, the queerness of God was incredibly threatening. Upon hearing such a threateningly violent wind, the apostles and others gathered around might have been expected to run away. When confronted with the great rush of the Queer, those of us who are queer will always wait to see what happens next.

The violent wind "filled the entire house where they were sitting" (Acts 2:2). The violent wind swirled round and round, tussling about all who were gathered. When we take the initial steps out of the closet of normativity, the queerness of God comes upon us and mixes us up. The queerness of the Spirit fills our rooms to dislodge us from our comfort with the walls and boundaries of the space. We are filled with queerness to the point where we are aware of only our own self and the violent wind of the Queer. As the violent wind swirls around in a moment of solitude, God fills us up and pulls out of us what was always there: the Queer within us.

Flaming tongues got loose and danced around the room. Why were the people not frightened when flaming tongues rested upon them? Maybe the people sensed they had always longed for a good lick from the flaming tongue of the Queer. Perhaps a fiery, heavenly lick is the only thing that can awaken us from our normative utterances to a place of queer speech.

"All of them were filled with the Holy Spirit . . ." (Acts 2:4). The Queer awakens the queer images of God that God has placed in humans since the beginning. By filling up the human vessel with an awakened reality of queerness, the Queer creates a queer space full of queer actors who have stepped out of their closets and are ready to accomplish queer things. "And began to speak in other languages . . . " (Acts 2:4). The mixture and utterances of diverse languages is a defining characteristic of queer spaces. The queers speak as God has uniquely called each of them to speak in their own tongue. In a world of normativity, the utterances of a queer are always going to be other languages. A queer is going to speak like a queer. Who are we to try and normatize the language of anyone? When queerness flows out of the mouth, we begin to see the image of the Queer flaring up from our very soul.

The Spirit makes the queerness that we hear coming from these various tongues possible. Without the Queer, there would have been nothing more than normative silence or meaningless chatter. God shows up and pulls meaning out of each individual. The people spoke and grew queerer "as the Spirit gave them ability" (Acts 2:4). God is the Queer doing the queering. God is the one pulling the tongues out of the people. God is the great queerer of every moment.

Devout people from every nation on earth were present to witness the explosion of the Queer. A devout person must make sense of the world from the paradigm of their particular sect of their particular religious group. The problem is that most paradigms are not God's paradigm. The Queer is always too queer to fit into a normative paradigm. The Queer was loose, and "the crowd gathered and was bewildered" (Acts 2:6). The scene was probably not all that different from someone jumping up and shaking their ass for Jesus in the midst of a worship service at a First Baptist Church in Mississippi at 11:15 on a Sunday morning. Throughout the pews, everyone is leaning in to try to figure out what is going on and talking all kinds of shit about the ass-shaker. In the midst of the spectacle of it all, there is a slight inclination in everyone watching that they want to get up and shake their ass too. The bewilderment comes from that desire to be queer too. " . . . Each one heard them speaking in the native language of each" (Acts 2:6). The queerest aspect of Pentecost is that the invitation to be queer went out to the nations through queer utterances of the power of God in the languages of all gathered. The Queer uses the coming out of queers to call other people out of their closets too. The violence of Pentecost is that closets are being spoken to and torn down with tongues of fire.

The questions erupted after the Queer got loose. The question "What does this mean?" features prominently in the text (Acts 2:12). Meaning is a normative impulse that pulls us away from the path of the Queer that is being. On this side of paradise, there will always be those whose primary ambition is to explain. Queerness is often unexplainable. Sometimes we just have to be. The crowd at Pentecost wanted answers before they came out of their closets. God was just inviting them into the light of being queer. There is very little difference between the ones who questioned and the ones who sneeringly say, "They are filled with new wine" (Acts 2:12). Both parties are trying to explain the unexplainable. There is a need to stop and be. The Queer just wants us to be who and what the Queer made us to be: queer.

Imagine hearing a symphony directed by God. Everyone is amazed at the beautiful melodies coming from each individual, queerly played instrument. The melodies move you to close your eyes and hang on every note. The symphony inspires you to be queer too. Just when you feel the Queer about to combust inside you, someone stands up in the middle of the celestial auditorium and tries to explain what is going on and set rules for the continuance of the symphony. On Pentecost, Peter is the great explainer.

In a sermon on the meaning of the events everyone just witnessed, Peter delivers an apologetic that Jesus Christ was indeed the Son of God. Was there a need to explain? The beautiful queerness of the moment must have been lingering. I believe this explanation is more about Peter than God. Peter has to explain in order to create meaning out of what he has just experienced. Would the Queer not have moved in the lives of those gathered with or without Peter's sermon? The beauty of queerness is that it moves us whether we can describe it or not, and no explanation is necessary for it to be. Peter also makes it very clear that the authorities are responsible for killing Jesus (Acts 2:23, 36). Excessive explanation and a dose of guilt were included in the first sermon. The borders and boundaries that define all of our churches are a direct result of this moment. The legalism and guilt-inducing nature of the church those at Pentecost first experienced flow through the first converts and on down to us. Through signs and wonders, people continued to be converted to a religion. Did the apostles miss something by trying to control and define the early Jesus movement? What if Peter had never preached that sermon and just walked down to the river to see who wanted to be baptized? What if Peter had just let the queerness flow without trying to contain or explain it? What if the people were encouraged to be rather than to doctrinally believe? Perhaps the queerness of God wouldn't be so hard to find now.

The Eunuch

Phillip saw "an angel of the Lord" (Acts 8:26). The angel was easily identified as an angel. The angel is identified as being of the Lord and not of anyone else. How were things so clear for Phillip? When someone knows the Queer within, they also quickly recognize the Queer without. Phillip knew that the angel was of God because Phillip knew the Queer within. The queerness of the situation is not lost on any of the participants.

The queer does not tarry when the Queer has spoken. For the queer knows that the power of God is found in pursuing the purposes of the Queer. Phillip "got up and went" (Acts 8:27). The restoration of the world would be at hand if we all would respond to the Queer as Phillip does. The comforts of closets hold most back. In the normativity of the closet, it is difficult to hear the voice of the Queer because the door is shut so tightly that it is difficult for any sound to get in. Those who have a queer ear to hear will hear the Queer. Those who are willing to step queerly and risk the slander of normative people open the door. When God called, Phillip took the steps of hearing, risking, and stepping toward greater queerness. The events grew queerer quickly.

The Queer speaks to and through the diversity of the world. Wide diversities of people traveled to and through Jerusalem. One sojourner was the official in charge of the treasury from the court of Queen Candace of Ethiopia. Thinking from our current cultural descriptions, Phillip was about to meet up with a very success-ful black man. The official is also a eunuch, or a sexual minority. In other words, Phillip was about to meet up with a person of an alternative sexuality and gender who is black and very success-ful. Those who are homophobic, genderphobic, racist, or classist would have missed him. Finally, we are told that the Ethiopian eu-nuch had come to Jerusalem to worship and was on his way home. Those who are bothered by public demonstrations of spirituality would have missed him. The Queer has destroyed many modern and ancient categories for prejudice and discrimination before we even get to witness what happens next.

The Ethiopian eunuch was "returning home" (Acts 8:28). Worship was important to the Ethiopian eunuch—important enough that the eunuch traveled over a long distance to worship in Jerusalem. Queerness blossoms when we are connected to the

Queer. Worship is an act of connection that takes on many different forms. The act of worship is both connectional and individual. We all connect to the source in our own queer ways, and such ways must be uplifted in celebration. Is there any denying the queer reality and power of a connection to the Queer?

Chariots were not available to people of little means. The Ethiopian eunuch was being driven in the luxury automobile of his day. In the posh, comfortable seats, the eunuch sat reading the words of the prophet Isaiah. In these circumstances, the Ethiopian eunuch is like the student on her way back from an exciting worship experience at summer camp who sits in the car and reads her Bible the whole way home. Like such a student, the Ethiopian eunuch had been pumped full of energy but now had very little theology to help understand the text. Sometimes we need other queers to help guide us.

"Then the Spirit said to Phillip, 'Go over to this chariot and join it'" (Acts 8:29). Who would have ever thought that the Queer would lead anyone to a place of luxury to share the Queer's message? Those who are interested in dehumanizing the rich will find these passages difficult. Phillip is told to take all his queerness and run to the chariot. Do you think that Phillip was skeptical of what he might be running toward? Upon reaching the chariot, Phillip hears something familiar. We can connect with anyone if we open our ears and hearts to hear and feel the familiar. The Ethiopian eunuch was deeply closeted, but his yearning for his queer origins was familiar to Phillip. Maybe the familiarity of the search for our queer origins is familiar to us all.

Phillip offers the Ethiopian eunuch an invitation to wider queer conversation when he says, "Do you understand what you are reading?" (Acts 8:30). Why did Phillip ask the question? Did Phillip hear the eunuch mispronouncing the language? Was it the way he was holding the scroll? Maybe it was that Phillip had the queer confidence that he could help someone push through the last vestiges of normativity to wider queerness. Normativity is easy to spot, and queerness breeds confidence to push against it. The Ethiopian eunuch replied, "How can I, unless someone guides me?" (Acts 8:31). Phillip did not force his way into the Ethiopian eunuch's luxurious closet. Phillip asked a question and was invited in. If we want to minister to people in their closets, we must ask questions that allow us to be invited in.

Proper pastoral boundaries would seem to indicate that it is improper and unwise for two people of questionable sexual or gender identities to share such close quarters in the back of a luxury chariot. Who knows what could happen? The queer jumped in, and the blossoming queer invited him in. Maybe part of queerness is jumping into the spaces you feel the Queer at work and making the normative spaces queer with your very presence. The two started to read together. Do you think one was holding one side of the scroll while the other held the other side? Who knows? Without a care about what anyone else would think, the two queers went deeper into the text.

The Ethiopian eunuch was pondering the prophetic words of Isaiah, "Like a sheep he was led to the slaughter, and like a lamb silent before his shearer, so he does not open his mouth. In his humiliation justice was denied him. Who can describe his generation? For his life is taken away from the earth" (Acts 8:32). We are still pondering these words. The consistent murders of unarmed black people by police, the genocide of religious minorities, the constant violence against women, the murder of transgender people, and the numerous other injustices that fill our planet push us to ponder all the humiliated lambs being lead to the slaughter without justice. We wonder the same things Isaiah is asking. What is wrong with us? How can we do such things? Why is everyone so silent? Perhaps the first step of the queer pursuit of justice is to be found in the wondering, and then the wondering pushes us to queer action. The passages that the Ethiopian eunuch read are quite queer. In each line there are questions and judgments about a world where violence, injustice, and humiliation are normative. In the same way that we demand answers to explain the normative evil in our world, the Ethiopian eunuch demanded answers about his world.

Phillip shared the good news of Jesus with the Ethiopian eunuch. What was the good news? The eunuch had it all. We don't need to forget that Phillip is riding in his luxurious chariot. If life is about gaining money and privilege, it seems to me that the eunuch had all the good news he needed. The problem is that normative constructions and conversations around power and privilege were not enough. The Ethiopian eunuch had a strange void in his heart that told him there was more. In a world that blinds people with power and privilege, Phillip poured the waters of baptism into the eunuch's void, and the Spirit of God did the rest. The Ethiopian eunuch realized that true power comes from the liberation of God, not the normative rulers of our world.

"When they came out of the water, the Spirit of the Lord snatched Phillip away; the eunuch saw him no more, and went on his way rejoicing" (Acts 8:39). We spend much time creating normative modes of religious practice. People always want to be the disciple of the latest teacher. The greatest teacher is the Queer that is in you. The Ethiopian eunuch went through no confirmation classes or periods of discipleship. There was no normatizing, dogmatizing, or regularizing of his faith. Phillip gave the eunuch the good news of Jesus, and God snatched him away. With the knowledge that the Queer was in him and was going to make him queerer, the Ethiopian eunuch didn't need the normative discipleship of Phillip and was able to go on his way, rejoicing even in Phillip's absence. We would do well to learn from the eunuch and realize that the Queer will always be the Queer in us.

The Lover Boy

Paul struggled with queerness throughout his life. Coming from a background of normatizing legalisms and dogmatisms, Paul simply struggled to live into the freedom and grace of Jesus he so often spoke about. We all know people like Paul—those who want to do good but who struggle to find the way. People have speculated about what Paul's "thorn in the flesh" was ever since he wrote about it in 2 Cor 12:7. Maybe Paul was a child molester? Perhaps Paul was trying to overcome some other unpardonable attraction. Maybe the thorn is something familiar to us? Maybe the thorny was something we wouldn't find so thorny today? Regardless of how thorny the thorn was, is anyone beyond embracing the queerness of God? Despite his sexism, homophobia, racism, classism, and a whole host of other -isms and phobias he wrote into the sacred text, Paul made many beautiful statements about God that teach us much about following the Queer. To dismiss Paul is to dismiss our self. For who among us is beyond reproach and judgment as we stand trembling with fear in our closets? Queerness is learning to find the Queer in all and seeking to cultivate the righteousness that can come from within. We see moments of tremendous queer love in the writings of Paul, and we must cling to those moments to connect with the queer side of Paul.

No Separation

> "For I am convinced that neither death, nor life, nor angels, nor rulers, nor things present, nor things to come, nor powers, nor height, nor depth, nor anything else in all of creation, will be able to separate us from the love of God in Christ Jesus our Lord."
>
> —Rom 8:38

Paul believed that the love of God was queer beyond imagination. Paul believed because Paul experienced a love that found him while he was a serial killer and pursued him through whatever his thorn was. Paul couldn't shake God's love, no matter what. The queer nature of God's love is that no matter how many times we pop in and out of the closet of normativity, the Queer will not let us go. Whether he meant to or not, Paul taught me not to believe in hell. I think hell is one of the normative thorns that Paul and almost all of us carry right now. Nothing can separate us from the queer love of God, and may we continue to grow until that day when we get to experience the love of the Queer in all its fullness. Though we all start at different points and experience different struggles, Paul kept working to become queerer in love, and so should we. Nothing will separate us from the love of the Queer; it is always there banging on our closet doors, reminding us of love's presence and trying to pull us out into the light of the embrace of the true self in the arms of the true God. There is no queerer love than one that is inextinguishable.

Love Defined

In spite of all the conflicted static Paul gives us about love and relationships in most of his New Testament writings, I believe the Queer within Paul comes out in 1 Cor 13. Paul said apart from love, everything is just noise, or "a noisy gong or clanging cymbal" (1 Cor 13:1). Paul has created no queerer standard by which to judge the self and others. The normative closet muffles love. To speak queerly, we must step out the door and into the light. We live in an age of prophets. People want to run around describing what is wrong with the whole world. You can call anything you do social justice, but if there is no love in it, it is meaningless. We have plenty of scientists, theologians, and philosophers to help us understand the universe, but if they don't have love, they are talking gibberish. There are smart people everywhere, but if you don't have love, you have nothing. You can believe in God and pray all day, but if you don't have queer love, then you don't understand the God you claim faith in. If you give everything away and sacrifice your body without love, then you might as well have kept it all. Over and over, Paul describes a life without love as nothing. In the process, Paul steps out of the closet and embraces the Queer for a little while. For the Queer is love.

We can feel the queerness of love in the words of Paul. It is almost as if we are making love together as we read about what love is and feel the words inside of us and know them to be true. From 1 Cor 13:4–6, Paul experiences an orgasm of expression in defining love queerly. Because he has actually felt them, Paul knows these words to be true and can speak queerly with the authority of the "is" and the "is not" because he has striven to make love with the

Queer. "Love is patient . . . kind . . . not envious or boastful or arrogant or rude . . . does not insist on its own way . . . is not irritable or resentful . . . does not rejoice in wrongdoing, but rejoices in the truth" (1 Cor 13:4–6). Those who have the courage to step out of the closet of safety and normativity can speak queerly with the authority of the "is" and the "is not," for they will have taken the risk of making love with God. If we choose to embrace the queer and make love, we will know through our orgasm of experience and expression that love "bears all things, believes all things, hopes all things, endures all things" (1 Cor 13:7). There is nothing queerer than making love with the Queer.

"Love never ends" (1 Cor 13:8). God is the orgasm that never stops. You can't make love with God in a closet. The space is far too confined for the enormity of God's presence. You have to be out in the world, spreading the queer freedom that is love. Prophetic words are going to come to an end. God will make all things right. Love will last. Justice cannot be sown in hate. The temporal magic and wonders of the present will cease in the full presence of love. You cannot outsmart love. There is something altogether different about a mysterious construct based in sacrifice. Love is truth. Love is fortitude. Love is belief. Love is hope. Love is endurance. Love is queer, and it never ends.

That which is partial cannot compare to that which is perfect. Temptations of partial normativities fill our lives, and so we struggle between the closet and freedom. What shall we choose? The temptation to be anything other than what God has created you to be will end. That which is not queer in you will be burned up in the fullness of God's love, for "when the complete comes, the partial will be done away with" (1 Cor 13:10). Those who follow the normativities of this world and constantly feign fulfillment are children. The games of children are to be played within normative boundaries and borders. The Queer invites us in our maturity to leave the games and restricted areas behind. The courage to be queer is the courage to embrace the maturity of freedom. No more games. No more normative boundaries and borders. Push out and be . . . queer.

"For now we see in a mirror, dimly" (1 Cor 13:12). We see the fallenness of life in the dim mirror. No matter how much we try, we are unable to completely make out who or what we really are. The queer keeps looking and searching in the dimness of the reflection. When God lovingly completes the task of bringing us back to our original queerness, "we will see face to face" the fullness of the Queer's image in our very being (1 Cor 13:12). For now, we stare at the mirror, seeing only a part of what is to come. The Queer pushes us along toward love because God knows the core of our being and what is coming next: "then I will know fully, even as I have been fully known" (1 Cor 13:12). The knowledge of self is the inner knowledge of God. We desperately stare at the mirror, praying for a queerer vision because we have a strange pestering memory that the Queer is there.

The end. The end is a frightening thing for those who believe the end is *the* end. God exists beyond our ending. The ending is the beginning of the restoration of the beginning in the economy of the Queer. The end consists of three pieces, "faith, hope and love" (1 Cor 13:13). Perhaps this is the constriction and construction of God. Maybe the Queer doesn't know the future and simply has to have faith that love will win, just like the rest of us. Maybe the Queer hopes that the universe will be put to right and continues to love as hard as possible until that is the case. The base liberation of both faith and hope is the realization of love. We declare, "God is love" in the both faith and hope that love is "the greatest of these" and will be made so in our world (1 Cor 13:13). Faith and hope are the queers that birth the queerest construct of love. In the end, the queerest of queer constructs come together to complete our queerness.

The Slow Queering

Jesus came to earth to show us a better world that exists beyond the borders and boundaries of wealth and privilege. Through a process of sanctification, the Queer unites the self and the other in queerness through the blurring of borders and boundaries. Paul came from a background of religious privilege. Regardless of his background, Jesus met Paul where he was, and together they started a process of queerification. The writings of Paul illustrate that the struggle to be queer is real. Grace and law do battle in every sentence Paul constructs, and sometimes grace wins. The victory of grace is visible in Paul's blurring of borders and boundaries.

Considering his background of unrestrained persecution of Christians, Paul does not seem like the most likely candidate to make the statement, "There is no longer Jew or Greek" (Gal 3:28). If we could have caught him before his conversion, Paul would be the one shouting on the corner to the rooftops, "I'm a Jew and I'm proud." What changed? Paul was beckoned beyond his exclusive understandings of ethnic and nationalistic borders to a place where he was queer and interested in sharing the freedom of queerness with others. In such a queer space, each person has value because they are the queer person God created them to be. Through Paul, the Queer declares that the day when anyone should be degraded or dehumanized based on who they are has ended.

Unfortunately, neither Paul nor anyone else in the canon seems to have a fundamental problem with slavery. The law regularly got the better of him. However, there are moments where the ongoing queerification of Paul bubbles up into stark reality. One such moment occurs in a simple declaration, "there is no longer slave or free" (Gal 3:28). This revolutionary statement of economic and social equality pushes against all borders and boundaries of class and power. The wealthy and powerful would and should tremble in their sandals at such a notion. Can you imagine the wealthy, powerful master looking across the room and thinking the slave serving him or her was now an equal? The poor and powerless are no longer to be enslaved by the wealthy and a lack of access to resources. The lines have been queered, and we are to work with the Queer within and without for the day when all will have access to everything they need.

The fluidity of gender and sexuality is not something Paul shows any understanding of in any of his other writings. The moments when the text makes statements that don't fit in with the rest of the normative narrative are the very moments when we can know the words Paul writes are actually coming from the Queer. Through Paul, the Queer speaks: "there is no longer male and female" (Gal 3:28). If there is no longer male and female, people should be able to be or perform whatever gender God calls them to be or perform. If there is no longer male and female, then people should be able to love whoever the hell they want. If there is no longer male and female, then gender equality is a forgone conclusion. If there is no longer male and female, then a family is a family, no matter the gender or sexuality of the parent. Exclusive borders and boundaries around sexuality and gender do not fit with the vision of the Queer that Paul had. Who would have ever thought that Paul is the originator of the queer revolution overtaking our world?

"For all of you are one in Christ Jesus" (Gal 3:28). I am not sure whether Paul had any idea of how immensely broad the queer love of God is. We are pulled to each other, queer to queer, by the Queer within to complete the queerification of the universe. When exclusive boundaries and borders of race, ethnicity, nationality, class, power, gender, and sexuality are torn down to bring us face-to-face with the core of our real being, we can follow Jesus, the queerest of them all, to the Queer we came from. In that day and in that moment, all will be made queer, and in such queerness, all will be right.

The Revelation of John

Either John is the greatest fictional writer of all time or he had an encounter with the Queer. I am convinced there are not many other ways to meet this strange book. The Revelation of John is the queerest book in all of Scripture. Even though there might be moments of proclamation contained herein that are not from the Queer, we should expect to meet God in the queer spaces of the text.

The words are difficult to understand. Perhaps there is a need to think in the way John did. We have to locate John's gospel in our context. We are queers. We must bring a queer hermeneutic in order to understand such a queer book. We have the ability, if we are willing to embrace the freedom. The God who is queer beyond all imagination is with us.

"The time is near" (Rev 1:3). The prophetic words of this are a present and approaching reality. The battle between the Queer and the keeper of normativity is afoot. We fight against the spiritual forces of normativity that threaten the very core of who we are. Who will win? The Queer is the "'Alpha and Omega' . . . who is and who was and who is to come" (Rev 1:8). There is no losing for the Queer. All normativity will be transformed to queerness. The Queer is the beginning, the end, and everything in between and after. Queerness is eternal and will bring all of us to the light. The boundaries and borders of closets will be destroyed. From the island of Patmos (Rev 1:9), John gives us a place to begin our own vision of how.

"I turned to see whose voice it was that spoke to me . . . I saw one like the Son of Man" (Rev 1:12–13). John stepped out of the closet and beheld the queer. Sometimes rejecting normativity is as simple as turning. The boldly queer encounter is like a stunning drag show filled with colossal special effects, with you as the only one watching. John describes the figure as possessing a robe, a gold sash, white hair, flaming eyes, bronze feet, a voice like soothing waters, seven stars in the right hand, a two-edged sword protruding from the mouth, and a face that shone like the sun (Rev 1:14–16). The queen called the Son of Man was ready to roll. The whole scene scared the shit out of John. Falling down "as though dead," John felt a hand on his shoulder and heard, "Do not be afraid" (Rev 1:17). There are many who simply cannot face the queerness that is the freedom of a true queen. Seven letters go out with seven queer lessons from seven queer beings that demand our attention.

"You have abandoned the love you had at first" (Rev 2:4). Closets can be prisons that make us think love can be confined to such small spaces. We pose in relationship after relationship and pretend that everything is OK. Nothing is OK when you have left your first love. The lasting effect of the initial fall of humanity is that we have all left our first love. We all run from closet to closet seeking temporary, false loves. We must "Remember then from what *we* have fallen" (Rev 2:5). The way back is through the realization that we have fallen and the memories of where we have fallen from. After all, we had to get in the closet in the first place. The entrance and exit knobs are one and the same.

Wealth is a normative construction that sometimes fools us into thinking we are rich: "I know your affliction and your poverty, even though you are rich" (Rev 2:9). We all know the plastic images of people smiling as hard as they possibly can in hopes that other people might believe they are happy. We are afflicted individuals who are desperate to fool other people into believing we are not. The closet cannot mask affliction. We will remain impoverished until we reach within, open the door, and embrace the Queer.

"Repent then. If not, I will come to you soon and make war against them with the sword of my mouth" (Rev 2:16). It is always interesting to find a "them" when you expect to find a "you." The "them" are those the queer being of Pergamum knows are teaching people falsely and helping people stay comfortable in their closets. We don't repent and come out of the closet just to save ourselves. We also repent and come out of the closet to save others. Through our queer being, we afflict those who suppress their own queerness. The Queer within is a light to all who seek light and an offense to those who comfort people in closets. The Queer promises to bring a sword from the mouth. The words of the Queer will indict all who seek to remain in normative spaces.

The words that are written to the queer being of Thyatira remind us that temptations of normativity abound. We regularly hear false teachings that comfort the closeted. The temptations of normativities abound. We are tempted to use the bodies of others for our own gain. All of these temptations take us away from our first love for the Queer, the self, and each other. In the face of temptation, we must fight back and overcome. "To the one who conquers I will also give the morning star" (Rev 2:28). When we receive the star of overcoming the closet, we can shine a light that can complete the queering of the whole cosmos.

"I know your works; you have a name of being alive, but you are dead" (Rev 3:1). People spend excessive amounts of time being busy. The glorification of business is among the chief sins of our modern age. We are like hamsters on a wheel who just keep on running round and round. What is the point of constant physical exertion? You can run in circles in a closeted hell of normativity all you want, but the door is still shut, and you still are a fraud. You can convince people that you are alive, but if you are really dead, what difference does it make? There are those who say that people are dying in closets. I disagree. Those who refuse to leave the closet are already dead.

The Queer is the God of the open door: "Look, I have set before you an open door, which no one is able to shut" (Rev 3:8). So often the lies of normativity convince us that there is no other way to live except in a closet. We refuse to look to the Queer. We refuse to look to the light. We refuse to turn. No matter how long we refuse, God is standing behind us with an open door no one can ever shut. All we have to do is turn and walk through it. So often we deny the queer name of God. We refuse to acknowledge and engage the Queer within. We keep saying no, and the Queer keeps reminding us that the door is always open. The Queer is the God who waits until you turn to the light. "I will write on you the name of my God" (Rev 3:12). May the name "Queer" be written on us all.

Returning to the closet is the second great temptation of life. There are many who want to live their lives oscillating between freedom and normativity. The Queer is not mocked: "I know your works; you are neither cold nor hot. I wish that you were either cold or hot" (Rev 3:15). The Queer desperately seeks for us to leave the closet of normativity and be free. You can't be both slave and free at the same time. God desires to free the whole person. If you come out to some and not others or pretend to be something you are not, God says, "I am about to spit you out of my mouth" (Rev 3:16). When you're trying to be a normative queer, God spits you back into the closet. Don't nobody want to sit in a dark closet, cold and wet and soaking in the saliva of the almighty Queer. Through queerification, God spits us back into the closet until we are purified of our normative identities and ways. Oscillation between the closet and freedom fools no one.

No special effects or exaggeration here—John looks up into the heavens, where "a door stood open!" (Rev 4:1). Does he have the courage to go? John's courage doesn't matter. The voice called out, "Come up here, and I will show you what must take place after this" (Rev 4:1). The invitation to the door is an invitation to be a part of the beautiful queering that comes next: the return to Eden or wherever or whatever we were in the beginning. The Spirit of the Queer started moving, and John moved too: "At once I was in the Spirit, and there in heaven stood a throne, with one seated on the throne!" (Rev 4:1). Queer things happen when the Spirit gets moving. John is transported away from all normativity and into the queerest of heavens to see the Queer on the throne of all queerness. John had to step up to step into something queer. Upon arrival in this highest of heavens, words begin to fail and queerness takes over. The majesty of the diversity of creatures is no distraction from the beautiful joyous shout, "Holy, holy, holy, the Lord *Queer* Almighty, who was and is and is to come" (Rev 4:8). The Queer has been, is, and will always be queer, and we get to embrace the totality of it all if we are willing to go to, with, and into the Queer.

John sees strange scrolls, animals, seals, tribes, and forehead stamps, all building up to one moment: "After this I looked, and there was a great multitude that no one could count, from every nation, from all tribes and peoples and languages, standing before the throne and before the Lamb, robed in white, with palm branches in their hands" (Rev 7:9). The Lamb of God, which is the sacrificial love of the Queer, is the only queer who has the strength to bring all the queers of the earth together. In one body, the people shout out in queer unison without losing their queer differences. The beauty of the body of God is realized in bringing people together through queerness and uniting them in the Queer. The Queer "at the center of the throne will be their shepherd, and he will guide them to springs of the water of life, and God will wipe away every tear from their eyes" (Rev 7:17). The tears have been wiped away, and queerness is all that is left above. However, the battle against the beast of normativity rages below the fullness of queerness.

The birthing woman brought forth life in the midst of agony. God protected the child and the woman from the dragon. Growing angrier, the dragon sought to destroy the heavens through the uniformity of jealousy and hate. Thrown down to earth, normativity continued to chase the woman. Normativity has been at "war on the rest of her children" ever since (Rev 12:17).

Make no mistake. There is a war raging in the hearts of humanity. God is fighting for our queerness, and normativity is battling for us to be just like everyone else. The battle continues until the end. On that day, when all things are complete, the dead are judged "according to their works" (Rev 20:12). God seeks to purify those who refuse to let go of their normativity and throws them into "the lake of fire" (Rev 20:14) to purify their souls and bring them forth in all queerness. The fire is not to punish. The fire is to purify the soul with the flame of love. God's love is a mighty flame that will eventually purify all of creation. The purification of the partial must come before the arrival of the perfect—the Queer.

John had a vision of the beauty that is coming: "Then I saw a new heaven and a new earth; for the first heaven and the first earth had passed away" (Rev 21:1). Queerness consistently creates newness. When we are willing to walk with the Queer, we grow to experience a newness of life that works with and within us to create a new world. The voice of the Queer declares, "See, the home of God is among mortals . . . Death will be no more . . . for the first things have passed away" (Rev 21:3–4). God is with us! We do not have to look anywhere but within to experience the queerness of God. The embrace of the Queer is the embrace of that which is beyond death. There is no more death because all has been made queer. The first partial things have all passed away. We read these lines with joyful expectation because we know that love will bring out the queer in us and connect us with the queer in others. Love can connect this queer-filled planet to bring us to a place queerer than our wildest dreams, where we will dwell with the Queer who created all things queer to begin with. "See, I am making all things new" (Rev 21:5). The Queer invites us to see and not just to look. We must open our eyes to the queerness flowing within and all around us. The seen becomes the unseen, and the unseen becomes the seen in a restoration of true sight.

"I am the Alpha and Omega, the beginning and the end" (Rev 21:6). God was there in all queerness at the beginning and will be there in all queerness at the end. Our story has a beginning and an end in queerness. Do you remember? "To the thirsty I will give water as a gift from the spring of the water of life" (Rev 21:6). We spend our lives missing the thirst-quenching presence of the totality all queerness. The Queer promises to quench our thirst if we will turn to open the closet, walk away from normative distractions, and embrace the way, the truth, and the life that is the Queer. We are the vessels that need to be filled. Will we stay in the closet of our thirst, or will we drink?

"Then the angel showed me the river of the water of life" (Rev 22:1). The essence of our physical being is water, and in that place our essence flows. The essence of our total being is queerness. In that place, the life essence of the Queer flows. The queer essence of both God and all of us flows together in the one uniting stream of the Queer: "there will be no more night . . . for the Lord God will be their light" (Rev 22:5). Queerness will be all that we have ever needed and all that we will ever desire. For in knowing the fullness of the Queer, all of humanity will return to the true, queer wholeness that we enjoyed in the beginning. That which is normative will all be turned to queer. Jesus says, "Surely I am coming soon" (Rev 22:20). The queers all stand their queerest and expectantly declare in a stifling world of normativity, "Amen. Come, Lord Jesus!" (Rev 22:20).

The Revolution Commences

The revolution of the Queer commenced with Jesus and continues today. Through engagement with the stories of the Queer at work in the early days of the church, we learn how to discover and tell our story. From tongues to sacrifices to murders to visions to suffering to reconciliation to healings contained in these stories, we experience both the magical and the terrifying pieces of the battle for the Queer and know that our world is not all that much differ-ent. The battle between the Queer and normativity continues to rage. Will we listen to the new words that the Queer is speaking and respond with the fire of the early church until the revolution of queerification is complete?

Conclusion

THE BEGINNING OF THE Gospel of Mary provides ample space for the beginning of the ending of a queer project such as this: "Will matter be destroyed or not?" (2).[1] The question that begins the gospel journeys to the heart of human experience. Will my matter matter, or will I be left to rot? The Queer speaks through Jesus in his reply, "All natures, all formed things, all creatures exist in and with each other" (3).[2] There is a unity of matter. The survival of one piece of matter is dependent on the survival of another piece of matter. The thriving of one piece of matter is directly related to the thriving of another piece of matter. Unity is contained within and with the other. To experience the unity of the universe, one has to join the unity of the universe. The Queer's queerness is the unity that holds the universe together. The Queer thinking a queer universe into being has created a cosmic space unified in its queerness since the beginning.

So what is the answer to the question, "Will matter be destroyed or not?" (2). It is that "all creatures exist in and with each other, and they will dissolve into their root" (3). What is the root? The Queer is the root. The Queer existed before time and space. Nothing has being without the Queer, and without the Queer, there is no being. The Queer is the essence of rootedness. The Queer is not normative because God created all things to be unique and is altogether unlike all things. When things are dissolved into their root, things become their essence, and since their essence is the

1. Meyer, "Gospel of Mary," 31–33.
2. Ibid.

Queer, then their essence is queer. What binds us together in the end will be our root, and our root is queer. To bring about God in our world is to bind queer to queer and journey together toward our root of queerness.

We matter, and we are matter. When we consider what the nature of our matter is, we are searching for our essence. Jesus says, "The nature of matter is dissolved into the root of its nature" (3). The root of matter is the root of nature. The Queer is the root, and the root of both matter and nature is altogether different—queer beyond description. The nature of our matter will be dissolved into the root of all nature. The root of our matter is the root of all nature. The root is queer, and the closer we grow to God, the queerer we become. In the end, we return to the beginning, and the beginning was and is queer. "Whoever has ears to hear should hear" (3).[3]

The queer rootedness of humanity is at the root of *The Courage to Be Queer*. This project began with an exploration of the queerness of the self—myself. Without an exploration of the Queer within, one cannot even begin to understand how the Queer is functioning in the world. We all have the ability to discover the Queer within. Most are too afraid to take the risk of opening the door and walking out of the closet of normativity. Fear is the ultimate normative construction. In order to be the difference that we want to see in the world, we have to take those parts of ourselves that are most queer and let them run wild. We only become able to recognize those queer parts of ourselves when we are willing to look at our history and deconstruct where we've been normatized. I believe that in the past we find the path to liberation for our present and future.

Daring to explore our past is not just about queering the individual; such a process is capable of queering entire communities by igniting the queerness of individuals. For so long, communities have been judged based on similarities, not on differences. The problem with such normatizing is that the root of the community is not the root of the individual, and the root of the individual is

3. Ibid., 37.

expected to be sacrificed for the root of the community. In such a normative process, communities create a situation in which the cohesion of individuals is based on their willingness to sacrifice the root of who they are in order to fit into the group. Communities based on normative similarities have a fundamental inability to advocate on behalf of individuals, if only because individuals are a secondary concern to the normative cohesion of the group. When people begin to discover the queer within, real community becomes possible through the uniting of queers through difference. We will never enjoy honest community until such community is rooted in the queer freedom of all people to express the queer root of who they are. I believe this is an especially important word for those who are interested in the survival of our churches.

The late poet Shel Silverstein expresses what most people think about how God relates to us in a humorous poem entitled "Friendship":

> I've discovered a way to stay friends forever—
> There's really nothing to it.
> I simply tell you what to do
> And you do it![4]

The God whose love is predicated on our response to his every command is a false construction of God. In Eden, things were different. The first humans walked around with the Queer in the cool of the day. The queerness of the first queers connected them so intimately with the Queer that the queers were a part of the Queer, and the Queer was a part of the queers. The fall separated our queerness from the source of all queerness. We live in closeted hells until we are able to reach back into our past and grab hold of the queerness that was lost. The human experience will always be about reaching back to grab hold of what was lost until we are all brought back to the future that is the eschatological fullness of all queerness.

The existential crisis Kohelet experienced is similar to the existential crisis the late Dr. Nancy Eiesland faced in her struggle

---

4. Silverstein, *Light in the Attic*, 132.

to find God in the midst of the excruciating pain of her disability. By searching deeply in her past and coming to terms with her own queerness, Dr. Eiesland came to the conclusion that God is disabled and triumphantly remarked, "the presence of the disabled God makes it possible to bear an unconventional body. This God enables both a struggle for justice among people with disabilities and an end to estrangement from our own bodies."[5] When we dare to locate God in our own person, we answer the existential crisis by naming the Queer within us and uniting our destinies with the Queer for all eternity. The call of the Queer is the call to name God through our own person. Throughout this project, I have sought to provide an example of what happens when we are bold enough to locate God in our own queerness.

When we call the Queer a liar, we are calling ourselves liars and lying to ourselves, for the Queer is within. Jonah participated in this foolish charade when he was running from God. Fyodor Dostoevsky's character Zosima in *The Brothers Karamazov* speaks of the danger of self-delusion, warning, "Above all, do not lie to yourself. A man who lies to himself and listens to his own lie comes to a point where he does not discern any truth either in himself or anywhere around him."[6] When we lie to, deny, or run away from the Queer, we deceive ourselves. Jonah's struggle to tell the truth is ultimately resolved in the answer that is the queerest truth of them all: Jesus.

The truth of Jesus is the same truth of eleventh-century Islamic feminist poet Wallada bint al-Mustakfi, who dared push against the oppressive patriarchy of her day and wore a revealing garment emblazoned with "I am fit for high positions, by God / And am going my way with pride."[7] The spirit of queer resistance that filled this poet is the same spirit that was in Jesus. In fully living into the Queer within, Jesus became different and made all the difference. Through believing in the truth within, Jesus becomes the truth. Jesus shows us that the Queer within us can both save us and

5. Eiesland, *Disabled God*, 105.

6. Dostoevsky, *Brothers Karamazov*, 43–44.

7. Project Continua, "Wallada bint al-Mustakfi."

revolutionize the world. Transgender activist Christine Jorgensen put it thusly: "I found the oldest gift of heaven—to be myself."[8] In addition, writer Paul Elie muses, "There is no way to seek truth except personally. Every story worth knowing is a life story."[9] The Queer calls us to seek truth personally through embodied queer experiences and then transform others with the queer stories of our lives. Jesus did, and we are called to go and do likewise. Dare we allow ourselves to be queered through the Queer? This is the question of our existence. We have to be different in order to make a difference.

Pentecost is something of a coming out of God. We each have our own coming out too. The interesting thing is that neither is the first nor the last time either party will come out. Queer theologian Marcella Althaus-Reid recognizes the coming out moment as integral to understanding God, writing, "the Queer God, calling us toward a life of queer holiness, has been coming out for a long time."[10] Until creation is brought to a queer fruition, there will always be more people and places to come out to and share the good news of queerness with. Coming out transforms you and the world around you through the one coming out from within you: the Queer.

The Queer in the flesh of Jesus activated and transformed the flesh of Paul. Perhaps the Queer in you will activate and transform me. Throughout my interactions with the words of Paul, I have sought to imagine the world Paul inhabited. Words cannot truthfully speak to our own context without an understanding of the context they come from. With regards to the struggle of life, I doubt that Paul is all that different from us. Theologian Jürgen Moltmann describes the struggle of life thusly: "The glory of self-realization and the misery of self-estrangement alike arise from hopelessness in a world of lost horizons."[11] Understanding Paul to be someone who struggled between the realized queer self

8. Jorgensen, *Christine Jorgensen*, 332.

9. Elie, *Life You Save*, 472.

10. Althaus-Reid, *Queer God*, 171.

11. Moltmann, *Theology of Hope*, 338.

and normative self-doubt allowed me the freedom to look for the queer aspects of his writings. During this project, Paul has been redeemed for me through my discovery of his queerness. I wish he had come out to me sooner.

In his book *The Orthodox Heretic and Other Impossible Tales*, theologian Peter Rollins constructs the final judgment as the day when all of humanity will judge God by the criteria God says will be used to judge us—by how we treat the "least of these."[12] This queer reimagining of the final judgment pushed me to think differently about the Revelation of John. What did John actually see, and how can we contextualize it in our time? Roman Catholic mystic and monk Thomas Merton aptly describes what is going on in our world: "Man is divided against himself and against God by his own selfishness, which divides him against his brother."[13] While the language could be more inclusive, Merton's words illustrate the struggle between queerness and normativity that John describes in the Revelation. Queering John's Revelation gives voice to the battles raging in our own souls and the Queer's struggle to fight off the constant pressure of nomativity. If we were to leave the Revelation of John as it is and demand that it engage our context, it would be easy to ask the same question poet Pablo Neruda poses:

> Enemy, enemy,
>
> is it possible that love has fallen to dust
>
> and that there is only flesh and bones swiftly adored
>
> while the fire is consumed
>
> and the red-dressed horses gallop into hell?[14]

When we dare claim that God is the Queer within us who fights for us daily, then the answer to Neruda's question will always be that the fierce love of the Queer can never leave us, nor forsake us. With such a revelation, we stumble upon the final message of the Revelation of John through a question presented by evangelical

12. Rollins, *Orthodox Heretic*, 90–91.

13. Merton, *No Man Is an Island*, xx.

14. Neruda, *Residence on Earth*, 241.

Rob Bell, "Does God get what God wants?"[15] If the Queer is within us, then nothing can separate us from the love of the Queer. The love that we share with everything will bring about the queerification of the entire cosmos. We will return to the Queer we came from in the first place. In the words of Bell, "love wins."[16]

"A conversion is a lonely experience. We do not know what is going on in the depths of the heart and soul of another. We scarcely know ourselves," writes activist and spiritualist Dorothy Day.[17] The recognition of loneliness is the first step out of the closet; indeed, it is tantamount to placing your hand on the knob of the closet door. Day speaks to the loneliness that fills all of us, and to the crippling fear of what could be on the other side that often keep us from placing our hand on the knob and turning the latch. Once we step through, we hear the great cry of the Queer from those who trusted the Queer enough to make love throughout the past, present, and future of the cosmos, crying and moaning out together in the theological cry of Robert Goss, "No one excluded."[18] Theologian Brian McLaren first taught me to dream about an orthodoxy that is generous. I don't think it gets much more generous than a theology of the Queer that excludes no one and celebrates everyone.[19]

"It was a source of constant amazement to Jesus that people drank so sparingly from so great a reservoir. They were too timid around God," sermonized Baptist prophet Clarence Jordan.[20] Our timidity around God has brought us to a place of a great need for the Queer. If we continue to see God as the great denier instead of the great provider, we will continue to destroy ourselves and each other. The path of the Queer offers room for the freedom of context that is the Queer within each individual. God has to meet us in the context of the Queer, or God is not God. The danger of drinking too deeply from the reservoir of God is the possibility of

15. Bell, *Love Wins*, 97.
16. Ibid., 198.
17. Ellsberg, *Dorothy Day*, 9.
18. Goss, *Jesus Acted Up*, 176.
19. McLaren, *Generous Orthodoxy*.
20. Hollyday, *Clarence Jordan*, 133.

man deifying the self. Theologian Gabriel Vahanian describes the consequence of self-deification: "man is even more alone and estranged from himself than he ever was before."[21] While the danger of self-deification must be avoided, it is important to realize that there was a time when the Queer in us was so intimately connected to the Queer that we could scarcely tell the difference. We are not there yet, but we must continue to dream about the day when the Queer in me makes me whole, the Queer in you makes you whole, and the Queer in us makes us whole. In this hellish space between queerness and normativity, I believe we are like poet Maya Angelou's caged bird,

> The caged bird sings
> with a fearful trill
> of things unknown
> but longed for still
> and his tune is heard
> on the distant hill
> for the caged bird
> sings of freedom.[22]

We don't know what it will be like when we are no longer caged by the struggle and can live openly and honestly as queers. We dream about what it will be like for the Queer to banish all cages. Until then, we must keep opening the doors of cages and closets and pushing past the struggles we find there until the freedom of queerness is ours forever.

Humans tend to divide themselves from others through constructed, normative identity. *The Courage to Be Queer* calls the individual past such constructed, normative identities to a space of individualized queerness. The only way to mature past the dichotomy of "us" and "them" is to willingly embrace the queerness in our own self and in the other. Oppositionality in identity and relationship creates violence. We must meet the Queer within so

---

21. Vahanian, *Death of God*, 230.

22. Angelou, *Poems of Maya Angelou*, 194–95.

that the Queer in us will connect with the Queer in the rest of the cosmos. May we stand with prophet Oscar Romero and declare, "I don't want to be an anti, against anybody. I simply want to be the builder of a great affirmation: the affirmation of God, who loves us and who wants to save us."[23] The Queer is here to save us from the wars we perpetuate against each other. As long as we are fighting on the outside, we are distracted from the war that so desperately needs be fought on the inside. The war between normativity and queerness is raging, and our only weapon to fight back is the love and strength of the Queer within.

In the midst of the normative death that surrounds us, we must choose life. The Queer stands with us in fighting for the abundance of life, for in the words of evangelical writer David Dark, "God conquers rather than sponsors death."[24] Though death might be close, in choosing to accept and celebrate the Queer within, we will discover, in the words of prophet William Sloane Coffin after the death of his son Alex, "the love which never dies, and find peace in the dazzling grace that always is."[25] We find life in the midst of normative death through the queers around us that are the Queer within us. If we will open our ears, God is still speaking through them and in us.

Throughout this conclusion, I have used quotations drawn from a variety of queer voices. Some of them might even take offense to being called queer. Regardless, I believe that God is still speaking, and we must name the Queer wherever we find it. "The spirit of truth and the spirit of freedom are the same, for the truth is found only in the presence of alternatives," wrote the prophet Howard Thurman in his *Deep Is the Hunger*.[26] The glory of the Queer is brought forth in the presence of alternatives. The small, queer clouds of witnesses we have met in this project are but a fraction of the queerness that will be revealed when truly no one is excluded and the queerification of the world is complete.

23. Romero, *Violence of Love*, 123–24.
24. Dark, *Sacredness of Questioning*, 15.
25. Coffin, *Sermons of William Sloane Coffin*, 6.
26. Thurman, *Deep Is the Hunger*, 53.

I never expected to embark on a project like this. Less than six years ago, I had my sights set on being the pastor of a First Baptist Church somewhere. Then the Queer knocked, and I opened the door. What has happened since has been nothing short of queeraculous. I really don't know how I got here. I just know that I have been changed for the better. Sometimes we end up in queer spaces and don't know how we arrived. But take heart—the occasionally queer evangelist Billy Graham put it like this, "The will of God will not take us where the grace of God cannot sustain us."[27] I believe these words to be true. The will of God beckons us all; I believe that if we step out of the closet and experience the epiphany of the Queer, we will be changed, and we will gain the courage to explore and experience the cosmos. Open the door! This project exists to create a model for sustained, door-opening queerification. In the end, there will be those who worry I have gone too far. Let me assure all with ears to hear—I don't think I've gone far enough.

27. Graham and Toney, *Billy Graham in Quotes*, 155.

Afterword

I AM BLACK. I am woman. I am priest. I am lesbian. Ostensibly, I am about as "queer" as one can be in this current American context. So at first glance, it seemed that *The Courage to Be Queer* wasn't written for people like me. I'm already "out of the closet," and I readily identify as having a queer sexual orientation. But in truth, my sexually queer, black, ordained, female body is still tempted by the allure of normativity.

The spiritual mystic Parker Palmer puts it like this:

> We arrive in this world with birthright gifts—then we spend the first half of our lives abandoning them or letting others disabuse us of them . . . under social pressures like racism and sexism our original shape is deformed beyond recognition and we ourselves, driven by fear, too often betray true self to gain the approval of others.
>
> Then—if we are awake, aware, and able to admit our loss—we spend the second half trying to recover and reclaim the gift we once possessed.[1]

The Courage to Be Queer is my awakening—my call to embrace and to remember my made-in-God's-image, true, queer self. As Jeff shared his childhood memories of encounters with his queerness and with the Queer, I recalled my own stories. Midsentence, I dropped the book and ran to find an old journal entry I wrote when I was eight years old. The entry is titled, "My Deam." Written in the unsteady penmanship of a young third grader who left out the "r" in "dream," I penned, "My deam is that I will make

1. Palmer, *Let Your Life Speak*, 12.

the world a more beautiful place to live in. My second deam is to
be a gospel preacher, and my third deam is to be a person who
recycles." It was so refreshing to revisit that queer little girl and
encounter the Queer in her. And when I returned to Jeff's book,
he reminded me that this queer little girl and the Queer are still
alive in me.

This book was also my invitation to read Scripture afresh
and to preach differently in order to aid others in unleashing their
queerness. My ministry is situated within an urban context working predominantly with African-American college students. They
are all "emerging adults" incredibly vulnerable to succumbing to
the evil of normativity. In chaplains' meetings, we use phrases like
"peer pressure" and "fitting in" to describe many of the harmful be-
haviors our students engage in, but those phrases lack meaning to
my students. The Queer epiphany model offered in this book gave
me new language to try on. When I replaced, "reject peer pressure"
with "embrace your own quirks, idiosyncrasies, and queerness," the
conversation came alive. As we explored together these notions of
Jesus transgressing against societal norms and Paul dismantling
normative gender-binaries, my students opened up to exploring
other people who were embracing the Queer in the Bible and in
their own lives. It's beautiful to listen to them explore these unique
parts of themselves and to hear them revisit their own childhood
dreams, but it's also takes a lot of courage.

As I've watched my students desperately strive to love the
Queer within themselves, I see how much courage it takes to live
into the queer model suggested in this book. The author notes,
"After you come out, people often have difficulty placing you or
finding you." I've pastored students who no longer have a place
in their original departments of study because the Queer in them
has led them on a different path. I've grieved with a student who
no longer has a place at his parents' table because he dared to be
queer. Indeed, I've wrestled with my own losses that came with
embracing my queerness.

But it's worth it! Being embraced by the Queer, being queer,
and embodying the Queer is incredibly liberating. Knowing the

Afterword

Queer feels like the joyful experience of having a dance party in the middle of your living room with the curtains drawn! It's intoxicating. It's life-giving. From this book, I discovered that having the courage to be queer opens pathways towards truly living into my dreams and that loving the Queer in others helps them find their way towards their dreams too.

May you share in Jeff's Queer epiphany and join in this queer lifestyle. May you use the theological framework he offers to help propel you closer to your own dreams.

May it be so.

—The Rev. Kim Jackson

Chaplain at Absalom Jones Episcopal Center at the
Atlanta University Center & Vicar at Emmaus House Chapel

February 2015

Benediction

Go now in the power of the Queer to transform the world into a place where all queerness may flow.

Amen.

Bibliography

Althaus-Reid, Marcella. *Indecent Theology: Theological Perversions in Sex, Gender and Politics.* London: Routledge, 2000.

———. *The Queer God.* London: Routledge, 2003.

Angelou, Maya. *The Complete Collected Poems of Maya Angelou.* New York: Random, 1994.

Anzaldúa, Gloria. "(Un)natural bridges, (Un)safe spaces." In *This Bridge We Call Home: Radical Visions for Transformation,* edited by AnaLouise Keating and Gloria Anzaldúa, 1–5. New York: Routledge, 2002.

Baltazar, Eulalio R. *God within Process.* Paramus, NJ: Newman, 1970.

Bell, Rob. *Love Wins: A Book about Heaven, Hell, and the Fate of Every Person Who Ever Lived.* New York: HarperOne, 2011.

Branch, Taylor. *Parting the Waters: America in the King Years.* New York: Simon & Schuster, 1988.

Buber, Martin. *I and Thou.* Eastford, CT: Martino Fine, 2010.

Buechner, Frederick. *Secrets in the Dark: A Life in Sermons.* New York: HarperCollins, 2005.

Boswell, John. *Christianity, Social Tolerance, and Homosexuality: Gay People in Western Europe from the Beginning of the Christian Era to the Fourteenth Century.* Chicago: University of Chicago Press, 1980.

Campbell, Joseph. *The Masks of God.* Vols. 1–4. New York: Viking, 1959–1968.

Campbell, Will D. *The Convention: A Parable.* Atlanta: Peachtree, 1988.

Cheng, Patrick. *From Sin to Amazing Grace: Discovering the Queer Christ.* New York: Seabury, 2012.

———. *Radical Love: An Introduction to Queer Theology.* New York: Seabury, 2011.

———. *Rainbow Theology: Bridging Race, Sexuality, and Spirit.* New York: Seabury, 2013.

Church, Forest. *The Cathedral of the World: A Universalist Theology.* Boston: Beacon, 2009.

Coffin, William Sloane Jr. *The Collected Sermons of William Sloane Coffin: The Riverside Years.* 2 vols. Louisville: Westminster John Knox, 2008.

Cone, James. *A Black Theology of Liberation.* Philadelphia: Lippincott, 1970.

———. *Black Theology and Black Power.* New York: Harper & Row, 1969.

———. *God of the Oppressed.* Maryknoll, NY: Orbis, 1997.

Bibliography

Daly, Mary. *Beyond God the Father: Toward a Philosophy of Women's Liberation.* Boston: Beacon, 1973.

——. *Outercourse: The Bedazzling Voyage.* San Francisco: HarperSanFrancisco, 1992.

Dark, David. *The Sacredness of Questioning Everything.* Grand Rapids: Zondervan, 2009.

Dostoevsky, Fyodor. *The Brothers Karamazov.* London: Wordsworth World Classics, 2007.

Ehrman, Bart D., and Zlato Plese, eds. *The Other Gospels: Accounts of Jesus from Outside the New Testament.* Oxford: Oxford University Press, 2013.

Eiesland, Nancy L. *The Disabled God: Toward a Liberatory Theology of Disability.* Nashville: Abingdon, 1994.

Elie, Paul. *The Life You Save May Be Your Own: An American Pilgrimage.* New York: Farrar, Straus, & Giroux, 2003.

Ellsberg, Robert, ed. *Dorothy Day: Selected Writings.* Maryknoll, NY: Orbis, 2009.

Gandhi, Rajmohan. *Gandhi: The Man and His People.* Berkeley: University of California Press, 2007.

Goss, Robert. *Jesus Acted Up: A Gay and Lesbian Manifesto.* San Francisco: HarperSanFrancisco, 1993.

——. *Queering Christ: Beyond Jesus Acted Up.* Cleveland, OH: Pilgrim, 2002.

Graham, Franklin, and Donna Lee Toney, eds. *Billy Graham in Quotes.* Nashville: Nelson, 2011.

Guest, Deryn, et al. *The Queer Bible Commentary.* London: SCM, 2006.

Gutiérrez, Gustavo. *A Theology of Liberation: History, Politics, and Salvation.* Translated by Caridad Inda and John Eagleson. Maryknoll, NY: Orbis, 1988.

Heidegger, Martin. *Being and Time.* Translated by John Macquarrie and Edward Robinson. London: SCM, 1962.

Heyward, Carter. *Touching Our Strength: The Erotic as Power and the Love of God.* San Francisco: HarperSanFrancisco, 1989.

Hollyday, Joyce, ed. *Clarence Jordan: Essential Writings.* Maryknoll, NY: Orbis, 2003.

Hood, Jeff. *The Queer: An Interaction with the Gospel of John.* Indianapolis: Dog Ear, 2013.

——. *The Queering of an American Evangelical: Sermons, Statements, and Prayers of a Southern Baptist Minister.* New York: McNally Jackson, 2013.

Huckleberry, Lee, ed. *A Beautiful Thing: Sermons from the Inaugural Festival of Young Preachers.* St. Louis: Chalice, 2009.

Jorgensen, Christine. *Christine Jorgensen: A Personal Autobiography.* New York: Eriksson, 1967.

Kierkegaard, Søren. *Concluding Unscientific Postscript to Philosophical Fragments.* Translated by Howard and Edna Hong. Princeton: Princeton University Press, 1992.

Bibliography

Levy, Jacques. *Cesar Chavez: Autobiography of La Causa*. New York: Norton, 1975.

Liew, Tat-siong Benny. "Queering Closets and Perverting Desires: Cross-Examining John's Engendering and Transgendering Word across Different Worlds." In *They Were All Together in One Place? Toward Minority Biblical Criticism*, edited by Randall C. Bailey, Tat-siong Benny Liew, and Fernando F. Segovia, 251–88. Atlanta: Society of Biblical Literature, 2009.

McFague, Sallie. *Models of God*. Minneapolis: Fortress, 1987.

McLaren, Brian. *A Generous Orthodoxy*. Grand Rapids: Zondervan, 2004.

Merton, Thomas. *No Man Is an Island*. New York: Barnes & Noble, 2003.

Meyer, Marvin, ed. and trans. "The Gospel of Mary." In *The Gnostic Gospels of Jesus: The Definitive Collection of Mystical Gospels and Secret Books about Jesus of Nazareth*, 31–33. New York: HarperOne, 2005.

Moltmann, Jürgen. *Theology of Hope*. New York: Harper & Row, 1967.

Montefiore, H. W. "Jesus, the Revelation of God." In *Christ for Us Today*, edited by Norman Pittenger, 101–16. London: SCM, 1968.

Neruda, Pablo. *Residence on Earth*. Translated by Donald Devenish Walsh. New York: New Directions, 2004.

Nietzsche, Friedrich. *The Gay Science*. Translated by Walter Kaufmann. New York: Vintage, 1974.

Nouwen, Henri J. M. *The Wounded Healer: Ministry in a Contemporary Society*. New York: Random, 1972.

Palmer, Parker. *Let Your Life Speak: Listening for the Voice of Vocation*. San Francisco: Jossey-Bass, 2000.

Perry, Troy. *The Lord Is My Shepherd and He Knows I'm Gay*. Los Angeles: Nash, 1972.

Project Continua. "Wallada bint al-Mustakfi." Edited by Gina Luria Walker et al. 2015. http://www.projectcontinua.org/biographies/index/a_index/wallada-bint-al-mustakfi/.

Rollins, Peter. *The Orthodox Heretic and Other Impossible Tales*. Brewster, MA: Paraclete, 2009.

Romero, Oscar. *The Violence of Love*. Maryknoll, NY: Orbis, 2004.

Sanders, John. *The God Who Risks*. Downers Grove: InterVarsity, 1998.

Sartre, Jean-Paul. *Being and Nothingness*. Translated by Hazel E. Barnes. New York: Philosophical Library, 1943.

———. *Existentialism Is a Humanism*. Translated by Carol Macomber. New Haven: Yale University Press, 1997.

Segovia, Fernando F. "Poetics of Minority Biblical Criticism: Identification and Theorization." In *Prejudice and Christian Beginnings: Investigating Race, Gender, and Ethnicity in Early Christian Studies*, edited by Laura Nasrallah and Elisabeth Schüssler, 279–311. Minneapolis: Fortress, 2009.

Silverstein, Shel. *A Light in the Attic*. New York: HarperCollins, 1981.

Thurman, Howard. *Deep Is the Hunger*. New York: Harper & Row, 1951.

Tillich, Paul. *Systematic Theology*. 3 vols. Chicago: University of Chicago Press, 1951–1963.

Bibliography

———. *The Courage to Be*. 2nd ed. New Haven: Yale University Press, 2000.

Tolbert, Mary Ann, ed. *The Bible and Feminist Hermeneutics*. Semeia 28. Chico, CA.: Scholars, 1983.

Vahanian, Gabriel. *The Death of God: The Culture of Our Post-Christian Era*. New York: Brazziler, 1961.

West, Mona. "The Raising of Lazarus: A Lesbian Coming Out Story." In vol. 1 of *Feminist Companion to John*, edited by Amy Jill Levine and Marianne Blickenstaff, 143–58. London: Sheffield Academic, 2003.

Wells, Howard. "Gay God, Gay Theology." *The Gay Christian: Journal of the New York Metropolitan Community Church* 1 (1972) 7–8.

Wilson, Nancy. *Our Tribe*. San Francisco: HarperSanFrancsico, 1995.

Scripture Index

Scripture Index

Scripture Index